D0043109

The Motivation Hacker

by Nick Winter

Contents

Foreword

I wrote this book in three months while simultaneously attempting seventeen other missions, including running a startup, launching a hit iPhone app, learning to write 3,000 new Chinese words, training to attempt a four-hour marathon from scratch, learning to skateboard, helping build a successful cognitive testing website, being best man at two weddings, increasing my bench press by sixty pounds, reading twenty books, going skydiving, helping to start the Human Hacker House, learning to throw knives, dropping my 5K time by five minutes, and learning to lucid dream. I planned to do all this while sleeping eight hours a night, sending 1,000 emails, hanging out with a hundred people, going on ten dates, buying groceries, cooking, cleaning, and trying to raise my average happiness from 6.3 to 7.3 out of 10.

How? By hacking my motivation.

The Motivation Hacker shows you how to summon extreme amounts of motivation to accomplish anything you can think of. From precommitment to rejection therapy, this is your field guide to getting yourself to want to do everything you always wanted to want to do.

Chapter One: Protagonist

Spark

"To burn always with this hard, gem-like flame, to maintain this ecstasy, is success in life." - Walter Pater, writer

The idea for this book came blurting into my brain on a flight from Pittsburgh to Silicon Valley. My ninety-nine belongings were in the mail, my backpack was bloated with few clothes and many dreams, and I had just finished rereading **You Shall Know Our Velocity** by Dave Eggers, a frenzied novel in which the broken-but-satisfied hero drowns on the cover (the book starts right on the cover), flashes back three months, and drags his best friend to Senegal, Morocco, and Estonia in one week to give away all of his money and chase adventure. I gave the cherished book to the woman sitting next to me, who had heard of it and heard me laughing at the part where Will tries to leap from a car to a donkey cart in Marrakech. I thought, here's a guy who lived so much in **one week** that it overflowed a book's pages and he had to summarize the rest of his three-month epic escapade in a sentence and die on the cover. What had I done in the last three months? Wrote code for 717 hours. Got better at handstands and pull-ups. Packed my moving box. Discovered that eating half a stick of butter a day wasn't good for my brain. My adventure count was zero.

I felt a moment of panic, as if I had let my protagonist license expire and now I would have to retake the test. I had planned this ruthlessness of work so I could finish my startup's iPhone app before my California move. The idea was to then move in with like-minded lifehacker[1] friends, do amazing things, and transform the ferocity with which I had fueled my work into a fire for life itself, but I had made no plan for how to build those new habits. Now I was landing

---

1. Hacking: doing something so clever that you somehow beat the system. Lifehacking: coming up with ways to cheat at life. See http://paulgraham.com/gba.html for more on "hacking".

in ten minutes, I'd be at my new home in an hour, and I didn't want this work-brimming life to fill it as it had the last five places I'd lived, or to return to the vampiric entertainment of books, video games, and Hacker News[2]. What could I do to change all of my habits at once, to go from single-minded startup man to lifestyle design hero?

I generated one amusingly implausible idea: to do all these things I had always wanted to do at the same time, limited only by the seconds in a day, while writing a book about it. I would max out my motivation with every trick I knew, with the two most important tricks being firstly to tell everyone I was writing a book about all these amazing things I would do, and secondly to set a time limit. How long does it take to write a book or train for a marathon? I had no idea—I'd never written anything longer than an agonizing sixteen-page school paper or run further than five desperate miles—but three months sounded perfect. I could probably fit in work and a dozen other deeds, too, because they wouldn't take that much time—just motivation. And I knew motivation.

Missions

- *Goal*: Write a book. *Requirements*: Write a complete first draft of this book about motivation hacking.
- *Goal*: Run a startup. *Requirements*: Stay on top of Skritter work[3] as cofounder and Chief Technical Officer (CTO).
- *Goal*: Launch a hit iPhone app. *Requirements*: Manage launch publicity campaign and finish fixing all bugs.
- *Goal*: Learn to write 3,000 new Chinese words. *Requirements*: Go from 4,268 word writings learned in Skritter to 7,268.
- *Goal*: Train to run a four-hour marathon from scratch. *Requirements*: Build endurance from 5 miles to 26.2 while increasing speed by 10%.

---

2. Hacker News: a news aggregator for hackers and entrepreneurs. http://news.ycombinator.com/best
3. http://www.skritter.com

- *Goal*: Learn to skateboard. *Requirements*: Be able to travel 10 miles on a longboard.
- *Goal*: Help to build a successful cognitive testing website. *Requirements*: Hack on Quantified Mind[4], present to 100 people about it.
- *Goal*: Be best man at two weddings. *Requirements*: Learn public speaking and pull off two great best man speeches.
- *Goal*: Increase my bench press by 60 lbs. *Requirements*: Go from 1 rep max of 150 lbs to 210 lbs (I weigh 140 lbs).
- *Goal*: Read 20 books. *Requirements*: Read 20 fiction and non-fiction books on my reading list.
- *Goal*: Go skydiving. *Requirements*: Jump out of a plane while screaming in terror.
- *Goal*: Help start the Human Hacker House. *Requirements*: Do my part of writing content, organizing events, and helping housemates.
- *Goal*: Learn to throw knives. *Requirements*: Hit a target from 13 feet, 80% of the time.
- *Goal*: Drop my 5K time by 5 minutes. *Requirements*: Run an official 5K in 23:15 from a pre-test of 28:15.
- *Goal*: Learn to lucid dream. *Requirements*: Increase lucid dreaming and achieve three fantastic dream missions.
- *Goal*: Go on 10 dates. *Requirements*: Go on 10 romantic dates with Chloe.
- *Goal*: Hang out with 100 people. *Requirements*: Have significant conversations with 100 different people.
- *Goal*: Increase happiness from 6.3 to 7.3 out of 10. *Requirements*: Hit average experiential happiness of 7.3 over the three months.

I came up with eighteen goals. Some I picked for terror, like the marathon and skydiving. Others I picked for excitement, like skateboarding and knife throwing, or because they'd be useful and fun, like learning 3,000 new Chinese words and reading twenty books. The rest I had to do, like giving the two best man speeches and running the startup. I wanted to make sure I did them well.

---

4. http://www.quantified-mind.com

For each goal, I decided on success criteria and motivation hacks to fire me up. I'll introduce these motivation hacks throughout the book, and they're also listed in Chapters 11 and 12. I estimated how long each mission would take, built a schedule that could just barely fit if I wasted no time, and grinned at myself in challenge. *Let's see what you've got, Nick!*

Techniques

A chef wields dozens of tools, from spatulas to potato scrubbing gloves. Every once in a while, he'll need the pastry brush, but every day he'll use a chef's knife, a frying pan, salt, and a stove. Like a chef, a motivation hacker has a core set of tools. I'll introduce these in Chapters 3 and 4: success spirals, precommitment, and burnt ships. Sometimes you can reach into your motivation pantry (Chapter 12) and pull out some timeboxing, but it's often best not to get too fancy.

And just as the chef who dogmatically used his chef's knife for everything would cook a terrible pancake, so would a motivation hacker fail to quit an internet addiction using only precommitment. No single technique can solve every problem. This book will recommend several approaches to increasing motivation. Use more than one at a time.

Self-Help Books

I've read some great self-help books that inspired me. In these books, the author writes about how he used to suck at something, how he epiphanied out and then worked towards a dream for years, and how now he's amazing at everything and it's all because of this empirically validated, Pareto-distilled[5], beautifully Zen method which he has developed and wants to share with you in small bites

---

5. The Pareto Principle: often 80% of the effects come from 20% of the causes, so self-helpers often suggest you only have to do the right 20% of anything to succeed.

mixed with inspirational anecdotes about how he applied the technique in his impossibly interesting life. I would consume one of these books, maybe create a To-Do to reorganize my To-Dos, and go back to exactly what I was doing while feeling great about how great I would be someday.

I actually have no idea how many people read *The 4-Hour Work Week*[6] and then start a business that gives them the freedom to sell their junk and travel as in *Life Nomadic*[7], then return to crush[8] being rich[9] while winning[10] things[11] and getting people done.

Looking back, I guess I did go on to take the advice in these books—some of it, eventually. And I guess I'm trying to write the same kind of book (mixed 75/25 with the easy-gobble one-year stunt book[12]). But if I try to make myself sound more successful than I am, or falsely credit any accrued success to motivation hacks undeserving, or tell you that doing what I've done is hard while winking as if to say, "but you're just the person to succeed where most will fail"—if ever I try to feed you dreams as though they were meat, then you shall call me out as a shameful braggart. I wrote this book as a way of forcing myself to live excellently, and to give good ideas on how to do the same to those who hunger, who can't subsist on wishful thinking alone.

Some of these motivation techniques seem like common sense, but they are rarely applied. I read about them, added them to my routine, and found them so effective that I wondered why everyone wasn't using them. *Some won't work for you.* I write about ways to find your own path, but I'm a 26-year-old American guy who works for himself, has neither debt nor pets nor children, runs barefoot, and doesn't know two things about what's going on in the news today.

---

6. http://www.goodreads.com/book/show/15388302-the-four-hour-workweek
7. http://www.goodreads.com/book/show/7062693-life-nomadic
8. http://www.goodreads.com/book/show/6474550-crush-it
9. http://www.goodreads.com/book/show/4924862-i-will-teach-you-to-be-rich
10. http://www.goodreads.com/book/show/4865.How_to_Win_Friends_and_Influence_People
11. http://www.goodreads.com/book/show/1633.Getting_Things_Done
12. You know, where a guy pledges to do something absurd for a year and then writes a book about it: http://www.wired.com/magazine/2010/07/pl_print_jacobs/

My perspective may be different enough that I forget things. You may still need shoes to walk your own path.

Motivation Hacking

Motivation is fuel for life. Without motivation, you can't get out of bed. With just enough motivation ("Can't be late again..."), you eventually get out of bed, but not before twenty muddled minutes of half-dreamt schemes for skipping out today. With a little extra, suddenly it's not so bad ("Breakfast!"). But when you have sixty extra gallons of it, you leap from bed as if it's Christmas and you're pretty sure that the big box in the back is the new Xbox. More motivation doesn't just mean that we're more likely to succeed at a task, but also that we'll have more fun doing it. This is what we want; this is why we hack motivation. It's not as simple as hooking up Xbox-sized rewards to every boring task, but it's easier than trying to accomplish anything without enough motivation.

Hack like this: first pick your goals, then figure out which motivation hacks to use on the subtasks that lead to those goals—and then use far more of them than you need, so that you not only succeed, but that you do so with excitement, with joy, with extra verve and a hunger for the next goal.

You can use motivation hacking to improve anything that takes time and effort, and if you get good at it, you might find yourself gleefully penning your opus in the morning, bike-touring Nepal during the day, rocking on guitar at night, checking up on your steam-powered skateboard business on the weekends, and scaring the locals with your laughter at the thought of how you used to drown out thoughts of the dreadful five-page paper with television shows about fascinating characters doing things only slightly more fantastic than what you're doing. Or maybe you'll just keep your house cleaner and learn a little Russian.

I don't know what happens when contented people try supermotivation. Perhaps they're just happier doing the things they did anyway, or perhaps ambition is a necessary catalyst for excitement. But I used to have no ambitions, and as I slowly fixed myself, they appeared. Maybe there are no people without big dreams, just people with their eyes shut. Some ask me about how I do what I do, and when I tell them, their eyes open wide. That gives me hope for them and for this book.

Stay with me, and I'll tell you about the best motivation hacks I've found. I'll show you how I used them to fill a life that used to contain only work (and before that, only escape). There will be funny stories to keep us both entertained and inspired. I won't zazz it up—life truly did rock during this project, and although I include just the most interesting bits to read, there was as much glory in hour two of writing each day as there was during that first rush of speed on the skateboard.

Ready? Keep your eyes open, and let's go.

Chapter Two: How Motivation Works

The Motivation Equation

Here is the motivation equation[13]:

$$Motivation = \frac{Expectancy \times Value}{Impulsiveness \times Delay}$$

I remember it as MEVID. Motivation hacking is the process of figuring out what you want to be more excited about, then coming up with strategies for manipulating the terms in this equation.

Motivation is what you always want more of: fire, energy, excitement! It's that which drives you to act, to achieve your goals.

Expectancy is your confidence of success. When you're sure you can win (high Expectancy), motivation is high. When you think you'll probably fail even if you try, you won't try—motivation is low.

Value is both how rewarding a task will be when you finish it and how fun it is while you're doing it. Working on goals that are important to you brings high motivation. Doing boring, pointless things causes low motivation.

Impulsiveness can be thought of as distractibility: how likely you are to put a task off and do something more pressing. When you have other things you'd much rather be doing, your Impulsiveness is high, and your motivation low. If there's nothing else you could be doing right now, then Impulsiveness is low and motivation high.

---

13. This comes from research into Temporal Motivation Theory (TMT) as done by Piers Steel. It's all backed up by a lot of empirical studies and papers. I don't know if it's exactly, formally correct, and the actual math is slightly more complicated (there is an additional constant factor in the denominator), but it seems to explain every case of burning motivation or burnt procrastination I've come across. Read more in *The Procrastination Equation.*

Delay is how far off the reward seems to be. This is often hard to manipulate directly: rewards are often delayed so far that we hyperbolically discount[14] them into worthlessness. But sometimes you can set yourself up to perceive Delay differently, thus scoring a big motivation win.

By increasing Expectancy or Value, or decreasing Impulsiveness or Delay, you hack motivation.

For an example of low motivation, look to the typical graduate student trying to work on her dissertation. Her Expectancy of success may be low, since she knows that only 57%[15] of grad students finish their PhDs in ten years, and *they* probably didn't change their research focus three times already. The Value of the PhD is uncertain, since she's no longer sure she wants to angle for one of the few industrial research lab positions working on peer-assisted tutoring systems, and writing conference papers is even less fun than she's managed to trick herself into thinking. Her Impulsiveness toward solo dissertation writing is off the charts, since there's a whole department of other fascinating grad student friends also procrastinating on their work by doing exciting things to which she is repeatedly invited. And with who-knows-how-many years left before she could possibly finish, the Delay of her reward is about as long as that of walking the circumference of the planet. Every bit of work she completes toward her dissertation will be due either to an extreme expenditure of will, a stern exhortation from her advisor, or a clever motivation trick.

What about someone bursting with high motivation? Let's look at the same graduate student working on her side project, a silly web game where players compete to bet whether absurd facts are true or false. (Example: "Blue whale aortas are wide enough for a human toddler to crawl through. True or false?")[16] She came up with the idea with a couple friends, hacked together a prototype one weekend

---

14. Hyperbolic discounting: we value rewards inconsistently based on how long we have to wait for them. Today, we want to go to the gym tomorrow. By tomorrow, though, we will want to eat pie more than we want to go to the gym. Our preferences flip. Read more in *Breakdown of Will* by George Ainslie.
15. http://www.insidehighered.com/news/2007/12/07/doctoral
16. True story.

when she couldn't bear to think about rerunning her latest study with more participants, and has attracted a small community of enthusiastic players. In response to demand, she's adding new facts and working on a feature where players can submit their own facts and rank others' submissions. She explodes with motivation and is having a blast—at the expense of her dissertation.

Same person, different motivational factors. For her side project, her Expectancy is high, since she knows she can easily improve what she has already done. The Value of building new features is high because it's fun and because her players and friends are congratulating her with each hilarious new fact she writes. Her Impulsiveness is low, because this is the project her friends are all inviting her to work on. And the Delay is low, because every time she makes an improvement, it goes out to her players right away.

Now, doing science may well be more important to her than making games. She may learn the wrong lesson and think she's not cut out to do research, because otherwise why would her revealed preferences be so out of whack? It might be true that she doesn't like research, in which case she should quit her PhD and do something else, like start a game company. But it might also be true that if she just put some work into optimizing her motivation environment, she could reignite the passion that brought her there in the first place. She could use the techniques in this book to pursue either goal, and she would likely succeed *even if she picked the wrong one*, perhaps never realizing that she'd found the lesser fulfillment. Motivation hackers are in danger of achieving the wrong goals. In a few chapters, after showing you the first three motivation techniques and giving some examples, I'll return to this idea with some warnings about carefully choosing goals, those risky investments of time.

Look out! Example avalanche! If you've gotten the drift of the four motivation factors already, then fly past this section. Otherwise, see if any of these common low motivation situations apply to you.

Expectancy

High Expectancy
- No matter the task, you know in your core that you can learn to do it well, so you look forward to any challenge.

Low Expectancy
- You want to lose weight, but nothing has worked before, so it's hard to maintain healthy choices.
- You have never been very athletic, so you avoid physical pursuits.
- You view yourself as a poor student who can't get good grades.
- You worry you'll never be able to find a great romantic partner.
- You think it would be cool to write a book / travel the world / start a startup / become a hero, but you doubt you could pull it off.
- Public speaking / dancing terrifies you.
- You think you aren't good with money.
- You can't drive / ride a bike / swim / sing / draw / do math / talk to girls / understand computers / cook / be fashionable / get good grades.
- You don't think you can be happy.

All of these things can be done with a little practice by almost anyone. When you have low Expectancy, though, your confidence is so low that you aren't willing to practice. You feel as if everyone else can just do these things without trying and you can never be good at them. You've learned to be helpless. I learned to be helpless at 16 out of 23 of these classic low Expectancy skills above. Once I fixed my general Expectancy problem, the only ones I still can't do are sing and draw, and I just haven't gotten around to practicing those yet.

The biggest hack a motivation hacker can perform is to build her confidence to the size of a volcano. An oversized eruption of

Expectancy can incinerate all obstacles in the path to any goal when you combine it with good planning.

Value

High Value

· You spend most of your time doing things so fulfilling that whenever you stop and think about it, you can't help but grin to yourself.

Low Value

· You don't enjoy much of your job.
· You don't see the point of school.
· It's hard to keep exercising because it's so painful or boring.
· Efforts to learn a foreign language always peter out.
· Cleaning your room is a chore you can rarely bring yourself to do.
· You'd rather watch TV / read books / surf the internet / play games than work toward your goals.
· You get burdened down and stressed out by a bunch of boring tasks.
· You fall asleep at your desk.
· You don't have a good answer to the question of "What are you looking forward to?"

When you see low Value in what you're doing, either because the end reward is not important or because the process is not enjoyable, motivation is scarce. It can be hard to tell whether something actually isn't Valuable to you versus when your motivation is too low from other factors, so it's easy to mistake a bad motivation environment for not caring and vice versa. There are several tricks to make a boring process more exciting, but much of Value hacking lies in changing what you're doing from things that drain you to things that fill you up.

The motivation hacker learns to steer his life towards higher Value and to have fun demolishing boring necessities in his way.

Impulsiveness

Low Impulsiveness
· At any time, there's only one clear thing that you want to do, so you have no problems focusing on it.

High Impulsiveness
· You feel like checking your email / Facebook / news frequently when you're trying to work.
· You find yourself distracted by entertainment after work when you said you wanted to be creative or productive.
· You have problems focusing on what you're doing, instead daydreaming or chatting with friends.
· You get the urge to snack when you're not hungry instead of starting or persevering in some task.
· There are so many things you want to do that you can't concentrate on what you have to do.

It takes superhuman effort to focus on a task when you're surrounded by distractions. But when you remove distractions in advance, no such effort is required: concentration flows. The motivation hacker learns to anticipate and eliminate distractions and temptations, making it trivial to follow through with her plans.

Delay

Low Delay

- You are always so close to achieving one goal or another that you never lack the urge to go finish something.

High Delay

- Whatever, that paper is due in like, two weeks!
- It would take years before you'd be good at guitar / Japanese / art / gymnastics / writing, so you don't want to practice.
- Junk food? Sure—it's not going to kill you **tomorrow** or anything.
- The thought of eight years of medical school prevents you from becoming a doctor.
- It's hard to save up money for future purchases because they're so far off.

We humans are built to hyperbolically discount rewards based on how far in the future they are. We all do it slightly differently as measured by experimental psychologists and economists—a dollar today might seem worth sixty cents to me if I must wait until tomorrow, whereas to you it might seem worth eighty cents—but it's a huge bias for all of us. There's no point in fighting it by thinking that, rationally, the value should be the almost the same now as it will be later. That's not how our brains work, and those brains will make decisions for us based on hyperbolically discounted values, not rationally recited values. Pizza now! Work later! Train for Olympics never!

The motivation hacker learns to structure goals so that the perceived Delay is not so great. Intermediate milestones, process-based goals, and willfully optimistic planning are his tools here. With the right mindset, success is ever right around the corner.

Note on the Research

I first read about the motivation equation in a blog post[17] over a year ago, in March 2011. The article summarized Piers Steels' book, *The Procrastination Equation*, which was itself a summary of the state of our empirical evidence about how motivation works and techniques for improving it. I started experimenting with the techniques listed[18] in the article, some of which I found tremendously useful.

I then took the most powerful techniques I'd found and pushed them far beyond their original focus of fixing procrastination. While most of these techniques are backed up by science, my recommendation of applying several of them at once to achieve superhuman motivation levels is beyond what has been studied. This may mean we're back into the land of authorial anecdote. But I think it's not a far leap from using *enough* motivation to accomplish a goal, to using *excess* motivation to have a blast doing it. I hope you will make this leap with me.

Willpower

There are several competing models of willpower. The oldest model says willpower is an innate character trait, and you're either a strong-willed, disciplined person bound for success, or you're not. If this model is correct, then you would probably know whether you have a lot of willpower or not much. If you do have a lot, then you can rely on it to carry you through the hard parts on the way to your goals. And if you don't, then you'd better pick out a smooth path to your goal from the onset, or you'll fall off.

A more popular model of willpower is that it's like a muscle. The more willpower you exert, the less you'll have that day with

---

17. http://lesswrong.com/lw/3w3/how_to_beat_procrastination/
18. I list all the techniques in the penultimate chapter, "Stuff I Didn't Cover". It's also worth reading these articles about interpersonal variance in lifehacking results: http://alexvermeer.com/beware-of-other-optimising/ and http://lesswrong.com/lw/dr/generalizing_from_one_example/

which to resist further temptations, but the more you'll have in the future as your will strengthens. Were this ego depletion[19] model true, you'd want to make sure you weren't going to need to use too much willpower at any given time, leaving your will weak for when you'd need it most. You would avoid Ben Franklin-ing out[20] by trying to do too much at once, and instead aim for a modest exertion of will as you pursued your goals.

A third model of willpower is that willpower works like a muscle only if you believe it does[21]. If you think that resisting a cookie will make you slack off later, then you're more likely to eat the cookie in hopes of saving willpower for working later, or to slack off if you've already done well by resisting the cookie. If you don't believe in willpower as an exhaustible resource, then the cookie has no effect on slacking off. In this case, you don't generate the excuses which sap willpower.

Some thinkers have suggested that willpower doesn't exist, that all of human behavior is explainable without invoking special cognitive intervention to override our natural interests. Psychologist George Ainslie's response to this is my favorite concept of will[22]: "the will is a recursive process that bets the expected value of your future self-control against each of your successive temptations." That is, will is simply the process of making personal rules for ourselves that will help us reach our goals, and how much willpower we can muster is precisely how good we are at setting up these personal rules so that the we always prefer to keep our rules than to break them. This is a learnable skill.

Regardless of what model of willpower the motivation hacker uses, she will structure her goals so that she doesn't need to rely on willpower to achieve them. If we can muster it, willpower makes up for insufficient motivation by consciously imposing values on our decisions. The motivation hacker plans to always have excess motivation. If willpower comes into play—if it's hard for her to resist

19. http://www.psychologytoday.com/files/attachments/584/baumeisteretal1998.pdf
20. Ben Franklin listed thirteen virtues to cultivate each day, but found that thirteen was too much and had to relent, instead focusing on one virtue per week.
21. http://www.ncbi.nlm.nih.gov/pubmed/20876879
22. *Breakdown of Will*, by George Ainslie.

a cookie or focus on work or wake up for a run—then this is a sign that she needs to do more motivation hacking or goal adjustment until that discipline isn't needed.

Willpower seems to be needed in one scenario: when deciding to begin. In order to commit to a goal, you need to deny yourself room to weasel out. Instead, you must design a sufficiently powerful motivational structure in advance. For some reason, this part is hard. If you have ideas for how to make it easier, let me know.

The one tip that I have is that if you can't bring yourself to commit to a goal now, then try picking a date far enough in the future that it's not as scary and commit to starting then. Then in the meantime, talk yourself into it.

You shouldn't overuse this tactic. Committing now is an important habit to build. Don't read the next chapter until you're ready to commit. You don't get many chances with success spirals.

Chapter Three: Success Spirals

Goals Afford Achieving

Motivation increases with Expectancy—confidence that you will win. When you know you're going to succeed, motivation abounds. When you think you might not be able to accomplish a goal, then motivation suffers. Fail once, lose some confidence and motivation, try less, fail again, and repeat until you've no hope left. It's easy to start sliding down into this hole, you fall fast, and once you're at the bottom, it seems as if there's no light by which to start clawing back up to the surface. Soon you feel as if you were born in this darkness: just bad at math, don't know how to talk to girls, can't manage money, clumsy, not a dancer, a shy person. At least your brain can cordon off these confidence pits, so that you can be confident in sports or writing or telling jokes even as you ignore the muttering from those hapless pieces of yourself which took their first steps down instead of up and have never returned.

The converse is true, too: success begets confidence and motivation, which begets more success, and pretty soon you're fearless on wheels or look forward to crushing spelling tests. To start as an adult, after your identity is set and your "limits" clearer, this is a fragile staircase and requires climbing, but it can take you just as high as the pits are deep, and quicker than you'd think. When you've climbed high enough that you can't even see the ground—when you've accomplished goal after goal without fail—then each new goal will be familiar, even if it's harder than anything you've ever done before, and there will be no fear, no doubt, just confidence. And with a little planning and a lot of motivation, you can climb as high as you want.

Once you've climbed several success spirals, you'll see those I-can't pits as the challenges they are: success spirals that just start a little lower. You can get to the point where even the craziest goals afford only achievement, and the question becomes not, "Can I do this?" but "Do I want this?" (The answer is then usually, "Sure, why not?")[23]

How to Do It

To start building your success spirals, first make a tiny, achievable goal that you can't forget to do. Setting a reminder for yourself helps. Then, track your success doing this goal. (Eventually, the tracking system you develop can be the reminder for goals in any arbitrary success spirals you're working on.) You don't have to shoot for 100% daily adherence, but you should have a definite cutoff, like 95%. Your goal also needs a completion date. You can't succeed at doing something forever, even if it's easy; eventually, life changes. You can avoid candy for one month, or keep the dishes clean for two months, or meditate every day for two weeks, but then the goal should be completed. You can always re-up your success spiral on that goal if you're still interested, or make it harder or easier. Often, though, your interests will move on, and you don't want to be stuck doing something of low Value just to strengthen your Expectancy.

The important part is to never weasel out of doing what you said you'd do. If the day comes where you can't do the goal, do it anyway. If it truly is impossible, then your Expectancy will take damage. If it's just frustratingly inconvenient and hard that day, then when you persevere, your Expectancy will grow—and you'll learn to plan better next time. Try to anticipate any obstacles that could come up, and then either make the goal easy enough that you'd still be able to deal with them, or include them as explicit excuses.

An intermediate success spiral might start with a goal defined like this: "I will run 57 out of the next 60 days, even if it's just for two minutes, although I'll aim to run for twenty minutes. I will set a recurring reminder to run at 5:30pm. I will place a run-tracking notebook by my bed to mark whether I ran that day, and to remind me to do it before bed if I still haven't. If I become sick enough to

---

23. Except when it isn't. I had to learn to be selective and avoid prestige-oriented goals.

call off work, or if I am injured to the point where running would be unhealthy, then I don't have to run." A beginning success spiral might look very similar, except with something easier than running, like brushing one's teeth or reading books.

Here is an example of an advanced success spiral goal which one should not attempt without building up to it: "No wheat or dairy for thirty days." This one is hard, yet it's recommended all the time as if it's a piece of cheesecake to accomplish. You have to shoot for 100% adherence because the point of the avoiding these foods entirely is to flush them out to determine intolerance. If you've done many dietary restriction experiments before, then you can probably do this one, too. But if you haven't, then this is like trying to make money as an amateur gambler: one lapse of your unpracticed judgment and you're done for.

My organization for success spirals is simple. I keep recurring goals that I might forget in my To-Do software, like journaling daily or measuring my bodyfat percentage every two weeks. Others I add to existing routines, like doing handstands before bed or eating vitamins on waking. Others are habitual enough now that I don't remind myself. At night before bed, I open my Google Drive spreadsheet[24] and quickly record whether I have achieved each daily goal (while also recording some useful self-experimental data). This habit ties all the success spirals together, and also conveniently reminds me to do anything I've forgotten at that moment where I would have to put a zero in its column otherwise. Now I can rely on myself to make progress on fifteen easy things and three hard things each day, but it took a year to build my success spirals to this point.

---

24. Google Drive spreadsheets is an easy way to track your goals: http://drive.google.com
Now for some goals I use Beeminder, which has many advantages over tracking in spreadsheets, but has more overhead for tracking many trivial things on the same page. More on Beeminder in the next chapter.

Where I Started

When I first set out to use success spirals, the only thing I could reliably do was work. I had put all other goals on hold for the sake of my startup Skritter, and in the evenings when I wasn't working, I read Hacker News[25], played Smash Brothers[26] with my cofounders George and Scott, and then worked some more anyway, since I didn't know how to get myself to do anything else. Previous attempts at learning this or producing that had always petered out. My brain had done its protective trick where it explained these failures as things that I would be able to succeed at later, once I weren't so desperately burdened with the destiny of my startup, and I made it to the gym on-and-off when George and Scott were also going, though I hated going and refused to admit it. (I didn't understand that the problem wasn't that I was that unhealthy geek who didn't want to become stronger, but that my barely sufficient motivation made it unpleasant to go.)

I then read about the motivation equation and the technique of success spirals and decided to try the idea of always accomplishing my goals. Excited by the idea of developing unshakable confidence in success on a broad spectrum of goals, I decided to set a lot of tiny goals, each of which I could do in a few minutes, and which I decided I would do at least six days each week with an overall average of 95% adherence. (The most difficult and important part of starting a success spiral is starting small enough that it's trivial to succeed—I probably started too ambitiously.) This was when we were running the startup from Costa Rica, and I was preparing to move to Pittsburgh afterwards and bursting with things to try. Here is what I set out to do:

- Skritter - study Chinese on Skritter for at least one second
- Write - journal at least one word[27] on 750Words[28]

---

25. Hacker News: a news aggregator for hackers and entrepreneurs. http://news.ycombinator.com/best
26. A video game where dozens of Nintendo characters brawl. Imagine Mario grabbing Pikachu in a headlock only to be shot by Zelda.
27. My mom the professional writer has a similar rule: "You have to write four sentences a day on your project until it is done. Hangover, head cold, Christmas, whatever. (Comas are exempt.) They don't have to be good and they don't have to

- Meaningful work - do some Skritter development, not just email or discussion
- Weight training - do at least one strength exercise, even if it's just an easy set of pushups
- No To-Dos older than 3 days - make sure no miscellaneous tasks have remained undone longer than three days
- Feedback limit - check email and Skritter forum no more than every 90 minutes
- Surfing limit - spend no more than 30 minutes per day on misc internet
- Anki[29] - do some spaced repetition learning system flashcard reviews
- Social - go out and be social at least 5 days a week

The social goal of forcing myself to make new friends was the only hard one, which was my main focus, since I was most afraid of it. Then, so I could track some more things without overloading my nascent success spiral, I added some optional goals which I wanted to do 90% of the time:

- Eat vitamins - so easy once the habit is there!
- Be friendly online - communicate with one distant friend each day
- Practice handstands - do one minute a day and record my longest balance time
- Be sweet to my girlfriend Chloe - make sure to demonstrate love in a way that she appreciates
- Gaze into Chloe's eyes - I read that this is a good relationship hack, and she has pretty eyes anyway
- Update goals - go through my Google Docs spreadsheet each night and mark my adherence to these goals
- Mentally contrast[30] goals - for each goal, spend a little time thinking about where I am vs. where I'd like to be

---

be long, they just have to be. The beauty of such a tiny goal is it gets you in. You almost always write more. (If you write four sentences, you can't skip your two tomorrow.)"

28. 750Words: a private online journal. http://750words.com
29. I talk about Anki and spaced repetition more in Chapter 8. http://ankisrs.net/
30. I later dropped this. It's listed as one of the empirically backed techniques, and it's proven to be more effective than just visualizing the success of your goal without

It worked: I overshot my adherence target on all of my goals and turned them all into good habits in just a few weeks. I had never had such success with building habits before! The tip which worked for me was to focus on input-based process goals (write for five minutes) rather than output-based results goals (write one page), and to keep the required inputs minuscule at first. "Do one minute of handstand practice" was always easy enough, and so after under six hours of total practice, I got to a sixty-second freestanding handstand. Some days the results sucked (couldn't balance), but it didn't discourage me or take extra time as it would have if I had needed to achieve a certain level of balance with each practice.

As my success spirals grew stronger, I experimented with adding different goals, and found most of them just as easy to habitualize in this way. I didn't always do it right: sometimes I added output-based goals that required a huge effort to stay on top of. Other goals were more a matter of changing unconscious behaviors rather than putting in enough time. I failed at adding the habit of photographing everything I ate, since by the time I remembered to photograph something, I'd often already eaten it. Too late!

And the one original habit of clearing all To-Dos within three days was not entirely successful, because sometimes I would put too much on my To-Do list and it just wasn't possible to finish everything in three days, especially since urgency only came with the third day. I had a semi-broken success spiral on that one where I began to weasel and reschedule things that I sometimes could have just done. I did get better at rejecting tasks after repeatedly feeling the pressure to do random things to which I had foolishly agreed.

Success spirals—backed up by simple tracking of success—were the key habit for me. Starting tiny, tracking success, and slowly strengthening the habit of building habits: this is how you tend your success spirals. Expenditures of willpower serve only to signal poor planning and a need to tweak the spiral.

---

contrasting it to your current situation, but it didn't feel like I was getting anything out of it. Your mileage may vary.

Where I Am Now

It was too easy, in a way. After a few months of building these habits, I realized that although I was learning a lot and living a richer life while raising my overall Expectancy, I wasn't getting very much Skritter work done. I was spending so much time studying and exercising and making friends that my work habit had gotten buried. I hadn't noticed, because I expected this to happen in Costa Rica and was willing to let work slide in favor of exploring jungles and speaking Spanish and learning to swim, and because the next interstitial month in Pittsburgh was supposed to be hypersocial. But when I got to Silicon Valley that summer and set myself to start seriously working again, I found it difficult to break twenty hours a week while keeping all of these other habits I had just built.

I decided to relax my success spiral on the non-work habits, putting them into skeleton maintenance, and to focus a success spiral on getting actual Skritter development done. I had an iPhone app to write! In Chapter 7: *Startup Man*, I continue the story of using success spirals for immense work productivity, using new tools and a more sophisticated approach. Despite the shift in focus, I didn't lose the habits I'd developed. After I completed that mission, I extended my success spirals technique, grown large and powerful after a year of practice, toward accomplishing the goals in this book project. Here is an outline of a typical day during the writing phase, before scheduling complications like meetups and adventures with friends:

6:00 - 6:10: wake up with the sun, bathroom, weigh, dress, narrate dream journal

6:10 – 6:15: breakfast of two raw eggs, a little dark chocolate, a bunch of vitamins

6:15 – 6:20: longboard down to the park

6:20 – 6:27: practice Chinese with Skritter in the park

6:27 – 7:20: read a book in the park

7:20 – 7:27: practice Chinese with Skritter in the park

7:27 – 7:32: longboard back from the park

7:32 – 7:40: second breakfast of milk + protein + creatine + athletic greens, a little more chocolate

7:40 – 7:45: wake Chloe up gently before her 7:41 alarm

7:45 – 7:50: practice knife throwing

7:50 – 8:05: journaling

8:05 – 11:20: writing this book

11:20 - 12:00: intense home weightlifting and metabolic conditioning workout

12:00 – 12:01: handstand practice

12:01 – 12:15: eat pemmican stick[31], stretching routine

12:15 – 12:35: lunch in hammock

12:35 – 12:42: practice Chinese with Skritter in hammock

12:42 – 12:45: shower

12:45: internet on

12:45 – 16:15: Skritter work, sometimes replaced with errands like shopping, cleaning, and laundry, or hacking on Quantified Mind[32].

16:15 - 17:15: only time allowed for email, forum, social media.

17:15 - 17:22: practice Chinese with Skritter in Papasan chair

17:22 - 17:30: Quantified Mind cognitive testing

17:30 - 18:00: intense running interval training

18:00 - 19:00: cooking and eating dinner with Chloe

19:00 - 21:00: catch up, social stuff, more reading

21:00 - 21:15: update experiments, then turn internet off

21:15 - 21:22: practice Chinese with Skritter while falling asleep

21:22 – 21:25: attempt to induce lucid dream

21:25 - 6:00: sleep (extra sleep to aid athletic recovery)

Before I built up my Expectancy, it would have been impossible to jump into doing all of these things regularly. I would have missed practices, stayed in bed late, broken my internet embargo, quit during the brutal workouts, constantly checked email, spent too much time reading and working and not enough on studying, and not gone to sleep early enough. At each point of decision to do or not do one of these things, my old brain would have generated a stream of

---

31. The original energy bar: a meat stick.
   http://www.grasslandbeef.com/Detail.bok?no=1210
32. Cognitive experimentation website: http://www.quantified-mind.com

rationalizations about how I don't have to do it or can do it later or won't be able to keep it up anyway or I'm too tired and had better take it easy. But with my current Expectancy levels, I already know I'm going to do it. I hardly notice these rationalizations forming, and when I do see one, it is easy to recognize and destroy. With a long history of realizing that I always feel better after I get up or work out or study or accomplish something, no matter how tired or sore I think I am beforehand, the generalized cue of "I don't feel like it" has been largely rewired from the "Quit" response to the "Do it so I can feel better" response.

This doesn't always work, yet. Sometimes I do skip things, particularly when they're not being tracked or seem less important or scheduling gets crazy. Sometimes I waste some time when it gets too easy and I don't need to challenge myself to accomplish everything, as during the editing phase of this book. I'm getting better at doing it without being formal about it. When I notice myself skipping something more important, I take that as a cue to add more motivation hacks to make sure I do it, since in the long run, that's much easier than trying to keep doing it with sufficient-but-not-excess motivation. When I find myself wasting time, I increase the difficulty by adding more pursuits.

The Sword of Last Chance

The tending of success spirals is a powerful technique, but you don't get many chances with it, especially after you consciously realize what you're doing. Each time you fall off the staircase, the harder it will be to get back on, since there will be a stronger voice of doubt in the back of your head telling you, *You couldn't do it last time, or the time before that, so why will this time be any different?* It's like breaking a bone: that bone will be weaker for years each time you break it, so you'll have to be move more carefully afterward. Most of us start with a lot of broken success spirals, the sight of which is enough to make us lose confidence in our current attempts.

Investor John Templeton once said, "The four most expensive words in the English language are, 'This time it's different.'" Your chances of tending a success spiral depend both on careful planning and on your ability to convince yourself that this time truly will be different. This book contains many techniques to help with your planning, since a good plan for succeeding at a goal contains many simultaneous motivation hacks. As for convincing yourself that you will now succeed where you have previously failed, I offer two weapons. The first is the knowledge of how success spirals work. With this knowledge, you should be able to see why past attempts would have failed. And I hope you can see how to make this next attempt succeed.

The second weapon is as sharp as sin and as delicate as memory. I hesitate to give it to you. Either you'll use it to slash a desperate path to your dreams, or you'll shatter it by forgetting, or you'll cut off some part of yourself that you'll never get back. I hope you will never need this weapon. If you're already good at achieving goals, if you're *not* stuck at the bottom of an Expectancy pit wondering if anything will ever work, or if you don't believe what I've told you so far about how motivation works, then you don't need this and can skip to the next chapter. But if you're as I once was, desperate and lost, then hold out your hands, steady your mind, and take this.

It's the Sword of Last Chance. It's time to fight. See, when you know that you only have one chance left to change, to become a motivated human being, to start walking the path to success now or be ever lost in the darkness of broken Expectancy, then you are unleashed to try as hard as you can. You will swing the Sword and cut yourself free from neuroses and self-defeating restraints. You will go all in. You will know that if you fail this time, even if it's by holding back some effort that you think you might not need, then you won't get another chance. This is the kind of desperate effort that you need to break through the chains of doubt of many past failures.

I took the Sword with me when I went to college, knowing that if I couldn't pull my life together then, I would never be able to do it. My friend Cathy remembers me telling her, "In a week, I'll either be happy or dead."[33]

But you're not going to take this Sword of Last Chance seriously unless you believe it's your true, final, tell-my-wife-I-love-her last chance. Let me make you believe it.

Self help usually doesn't work. You flit from book to blog to friendly tip, idly trying to improve and sometimes making a decent effort on some strategy that sounds exciting. When these attempts fail, you lose a little Expectancy that the next attempt will work. Chew through enough self-help advice without swallowing and soon you'll be sustaining yourself only on the fleeting taste of inspiration, fantasizing success in place of pursuing it.

Losing Expectancy is a slow process, because your brain is good at defending yourself:

• The Slow Carb diet worked for a month, so I could probably do it again but for real this time.

• The Autopilot Schedule just doesn't work for me.

• As soon as work is less crazy, I'll definitely get in shape.

• I'll use a better tool to block reddit next time.

• I'll try harder at making friends when I switch jobs.

33. More on this in the Chapter 5: *Social Skills.*

• My friend told me about this dating book which was much better than *The Game*, so I'll do that next time.

These rationalizations dilute the impact of failures, and they dilute future efforts, since you can always find a reason why it wasn't your fault and another thing to half-try next time.

If you realize the implications of this Expectancy model and the mechanics of success and failure spirals, though, then these rationalizations lose power. The harder you try, the more likely you are to succeed, but the more Expectancy you will lose if you fail. If you are facing a goal difficult enough to require all your effort, then you stand to risk all future possibility of success if you try hard but not hard enough. If you fail, those rationalizations will not work. Your bone will be broken, your success spiral shattered, and your remaining Expectancy gone, and you will know it. You won't be able to tell yourself that it was just because you didn't try or because you didn't have the right technique, and that you'll try harder with a better method next time. So you'd better succeed this time. This is why I have given you the Sword: a sharp manifestation of the realization that this is your last chance.

You have three choices. You can steel your resolve and swing the Sword, putting together a motivation plan so powerful that there is no chance of failure. The scary and hard part comes now: committing to such a plan, leaving yourself no retreat. The Sword in your hand is there to remind you of the stakes.

Or, you can lock the Sword away until the time is right. If you're reading this at a truly bad time for taking action, then pick it up again at a better time and commit then. But do not do it lightly: most of the reasons for avoiding commitment now are deadly excuses. If you can't make a motivation hacking plan right now, then figure out an exact date when you can commit, create a reminder for yourself, and commit to taking up the Sword then without further delay. While you're waiting to begin, talk yourself into it. Do not postpone a second time.

Your last choice is to throw the Sword of Last Chance away while looking cool and expressing disbelief that this is your last chance. Perhaps it's not. Perhaps you already are a motivation hero who knows how to accomplish goals and is reading this book to pick up useful motivation hacks rather than to fix weaknesses. Or perhaps you don't believe in this model of Expectancy[34], either because you credit different science on the subject, or because your brain has generated enough rationalizations to convince you that you don't need to believe it. If you don't believe it, please prove it to yourself by writing down a short explanation of how I'm wrong. Then, please help to correct me by emailing the explanation to nick@skritter.com (all privacy assured).

It's terrifying to only have one chance left, but it's also exhilarating. As you make your decision to act, you can feel the confidence flowing into you. Your brow furrows. Your back straightens. Your jaw tightens, and your eyes narrow. It's time to be the hero of your story. It's unfortunate that your heroism will be a somewhat abstract effort of planning many motivational hacks instead of dashing through a burning building scooping up children or slugging criminals to defend the innocent, since you don't come equipped with adrenal glands that fire when you sit down at your computer to map out goals. I find that it helps to imagine oneself as a heroic Rocky-Mulan-Churchill-dragon-warrior preparing for battle. Take up your Sword.

---

34. Specifically, that repeated failures lead to lowered self-confidence which lead to not trying, and that this feedback loop can damage your motivation so badly that you'll need a heroic effort to reverse the trend and try hard enough to start succeeding again.

Chapter Four: Precommitment

Skydiving Challenge

I twice rode the Mystery Mine Ride at the Mall of America, where they sit you in a theater with a chair that lurches along with a short film of a truck careening down a mountain. Twice they had to stop the ride for everyone so some wimp could escape. It was the same guy each time! I mean, come on—how terrified of heights do you have to be before you'd rather flee the theater in public shame—twice—than sit there with your eyes closed for ten minutes until it was over? And why would you try it again after what happened the first time?

Well, I can't remember why I thought I'd be braver the second time, but the terror I felt is still clear today—and it's much stronger than the embarrassment of being that wimpy guy who stopped the ride twice. They had a kiddie roller coaster at the Renaissance festivals in the summers, and listening to the tiny kids' Doppler laughter coming from that ten-foot-tall dragon loop made me try it once. That was enough to make me stay clear of roller coasters for the next ten years. I went to Cedar Point with my startup cofounders, and they somehow convinced me to ride the Millennium Force, just once. The two hours of waiting in line between the decision and the consequences helped, as did the inability to quit once the roller coaster started moving. I have a picture of myself sitting next to our inexcusably younger intern Maksym, who is smiling that blissful wind-tunnel smile. I am screaming that scream from the famous painting[35], plus tears snotting all over my face. "Not screaming in enjoyment, but screaming like you're dying!" as one friend said afterward. Yup, still afraid of heights.

When I was brainstorming the goals for this book, I wrote "skydiving" as a joke. That night, Chloe's friends sent her a deal on

---

35. The Scream, painted by Edvard Munch in 1893.

skydiving. She's even more afraid of heights than I am, but she was on day two of a thirty-day challenge to say yes to every invitation she could. I could see her teetering on the fence, and I nudged her: "If you do it, I'll do it to support you." *(She'll never do it.)* She nudged me, "You could put it in your book!" and I nudged back, "We just have to do it sometime in the next three months—easy!" and so on until we fell off the fence onto the side containing two coupons for terror. We looked at each other. "Oh fuuuuuuuuuck," she said.

With skydiving, the scariest part is the initial jump, and you can give up right before that. It's no big deal, even—lots of people chicken out at the last moment. With the Mystery Mine Ride and the roller coaster, it's easy to get started: you sit down, they strap you in, and you have a couple minutes to settle in and wonder how terrifying it can actually be. And it's hard, or even impossible, to back out after the easy part. But skydiving would give me an easy out when I would most want to take it, and it would be about ninety times scarier than anything I had tricked myself into doing before. If I was going to jump out of a plane, I would need motivation stronger than my worst fear. And if I wanted to "enjoy the experience" and not "survive the torture," then my motivation would have to be far stronger than my fear, like a sumo wrestler facing an army of five-year-olds[36].

Precommitment

Precommitment, also known as using a commitment device[37], is a versatile set of tools for increasing motivation in almost any situation. To precommit is to choose now to limit your options later, preventing yourself from making the wrong choice in the face of temptation. Publicly announcing your goal is a common form of precommitment.

---

36. http://www.howmanyfiveyearoldscouldyoutakeinafight.com/ — and a sumo wrestler could also handle twelve-year-olds: http://www.mcsweeneys.net/articles/a-realistic-assessment-of-how-many-12-year-olds-i-could-beat-up-before-they-overtook-me

37. A dozen synonyms are listed here: http://blog.beeminder.com/synonyms/

Precommitment reduces Impulsiveness in the moment. You want to bring near the consequences of not pursuing a long-term reward in the form of a broken commitment if you stray off track. Instead of choosing between a cigarette now and good health years later, you have to choose between a cigarette now and being able to tell your friend you're still clean. Or you can easily resist the temptation of a short-term reward by removing it as an option in advance, like not keeping any junk food in your house.

Precommitment is an almost arbitrarily powerful motivation tool. You can use it as weakly as thinking to yourself, "I'm not going to have any dessert at lunch. Well, not any cake. Maybe if they have apple pie, I can have some, since they don't make that often. Or cherry turnovers. But no cake." Or you can max it out and use a commitment contract: bind yourself to give your entire bank account to The Church of Scientology if you are discovered by any member of a team of private detectives to have knowingly eaten any foodstuff with more than 10% of calories from sugar between now and your cousin's wedding on July 18, unless the wedding is called off (and not because of any plot on your part) or two doctors judge that the sugar becomes medically necessary for your survival. Even weak forms can be useful (although weaseling too much can backfire, lessening your bond with yourself), but the stronger the commitment[38] you make, and the less weasel room you give yourself, the more motivation you'll have.

You may object to motivating yourself from fear of punishment, which could feel terrible, but that's not how it usually works when you do it right. What you want to do is motivate yourself with extremely high confidence of success, which will feel great. Remember the motivation equation? MEVID: $M = EV / ID$, or Motivation = Expectancy times Value over Impulsiveness times Delay. Motivation increases as Expectancy of success increases, and

---

38. Neurologist Oliver Sacks once decided to kill himself if his first book was not finished in ten days (and he had hardly written anything). This is a strong commitment, but perhaps not a credible threat: if he thought he might not actually kill himself, he could weasel out of writing. He finished the book in nine days, though. From a RadioLab interview: http://www.radiolab.org/2011/mar/08/me-myself-and-muse/

more motivation makes life more fun. The resulting confidence and enjoyment are usually what make you succeed. Yes, if something goes horribly wrong, then the fear of failure from the precommitment will help you succeed anyway, though it may be unpleasant. But your goal is to minimize the likelihood of it even coming to that through careful planning. If precommitment is traditionally an Impulsiveness hack, then the way I suggest doing it may be thought of pre-overcommitment, where you're hacking Expectancy now since you know Impulsiveness won't get you later. You feel confident the whole time, and it's not about the stakes.

The more difficult the goal, then the more care you'll take when choosing your precommitment. If you just want to make sure you go running before dinner, then perhaps you'll just tell your dinner partner to call you out if you didn't go running. But if you want to quit smoking for real this time, then you are going to need to precommit to doing whatever terrifies you the most if you fail, and to find an inescapable way to make sure you can't cheat without detection. Willpower will desert you when you need it most, so you need enough precommitment to succeed even without any.

Binding yourself is not that complicated and doesn't take long, but the actual moment of precommitting is scarier than it sounds[39]. (After you commit, it's not scary at all.) Don't be scared into weakening the resolution. You should bind yourself with something far beyond the scope of the goal you're trying to accomplish, so that there's no contest: your motivation should be much higher than needed to get the job done, both so that you don't fall a little short, and so that you have more fun. If the thought of losing $100 can motivate you to go to the gym three times a week for a month, then bind yourself with $1000 and watch yourself run cheerfully to the gym through the cold rain that you hadn't planned for. If the goal excites you and the motivation is there, then there will be a fire inside you to keep you warm, and the rain and the cold will be puny obstacles for you to pulverize in your new hero boots.

---

39. Fortunately, the longer the delay between precommitment and choice, the easier it is to precommit, since you hyperbolically discount the short-term reward more the later it is. So precommit early enough, and it's no problem.

Skydiving Solution

I'm writing this chapter about precommitment and skydiving on the fourth day of this project. The actual skydive is at least a month away, maybe two. Not too scary at this distance—I'm only trembling a little. What precommitment devices shall I use? Everything I can think of!

1. I'll give away $7,290 if I don't do it on or before August 25, 2012. (I put another $7,290 on finishing the first draft of this book by then.)

2. I've already told Chloe, her friends, all my Human Hacker Housemates, and a bunch of people at a party. I'll tell my startup cofounders, and I'll post it on Twitter, Facebook, and Google+. (I don't like using social networks, but I haven't set up an appropriate public blog yet, and I need to do this right now.)

3. I'm writing this whole chapter about it in advance, and it would be terribly inconvenient to have to rewrite it with a weaker example, and to fail at something when I'm writing a book about how to do the opposite. (Every little bit helps.)

4. I already paid for it.

5. Chloe is counting on me.

6. I'll nonchalantly email my twin brother, who went skydiving no problem, and tell him that I'm going to go skydiving as if it's no problem, too.

7. I'll fix the date of the skydive now, so that there's no chance of scheduling problems. (Friends' schedules dictate August 19.)

Some of these things will motivate me less, and some more. I feel most nervous about binding all that money, so I'd better do it right now before I talk myself down... done, and I'm no longer nervous. I'll set up the other things now, too. It's important to commit now, not later. Hyperbolic discounting makes it easier to commit the further in advance you do it, and you also want to avoid the habit of putting off commitment (as Chloe always tells me). If you can't do something now, then set a specific time at which you will decide to either do it then or to never do it.

Now that I've precommitted far more than necessary, I'm so sure that I'm going to successfully jump out of the plane that I'm not afraid any more. I'm excited. See my smile! If only fourteen-year-old Nick cowering before the kiddie coaster could see it—now there's a guy who could have used some hope.

Beeminder

Precommitting is simple when there's a single moment of success or failure. You turn it into do-or-die moment, and then you don't die. But many goals are neither achieved with one jump nor failed with one drink. What about losing thirty pounds or finishing a dissertation? You need to make steady progress toward your goal by making far more good choices than bad ones, even while the end result is still months away, hyperbolically discounted until it's less important than a bagel or a round of Call of Duty.[40] If you precommitted to losing thirty pounds by July 18, then by the time you hit July 1 and realized you'd only lost ten, your retripled efforts would still be too late, you'd miss your goal, and the Scientologists would get to spend your money on more Mark VII Super Quantum E-meters.

To assure success on goals like this, you would have to dilute your commitment to something meaninglessly easy, or to commit to some reliable behavior (eating no desserts) instead of the result you actually want (losing weight), allowing you to "succeed" in eating no desserts by chomping delicious pasta instead.

The solution is to precommit to staying on track toward your goal at all times, not just by the end. You need 500 more words on your dissertation every day, and you need to be down at least one pound every two weeks. If ever you fall short, you die. When your weight is in the danger zone two weeks in, you'll see the reincarnated thetan of L. Ron Hubbard[41] staring at you through the

---

40. Call of Duty: the latest ultra-violent first person shooter where all the kids are playing more than a millennium per day.

41. I wanted to say "the mad alien god Xenu", but I guess Scientologists actually cast him as the bad guy; he wouldn't get your money because he's locked up in an

hole in that bagel. *Yesss, consssume carbohydrates. Your money is mine on Monday.* You'll toss that cursed bagel, and you'll soon learn to keep ahead of your goal so that you don't have to put up with the pressure. Then by the end, there is no crunch time—only success assured, weight lost, and a dissertation complete.

There are some complexities to this. Weight fluctuates. Words come slowly at first. You may need to abort your scuba-certification goal if you realize that you hate scuba diving, or you might need to adjust the number of songs you're writing per week if they're taking too long. You want to know exactly what you have to do and by when, but to have some reasonable leeway built in. You want escape clauses. You want the ability to adjust the goal if needed, but not just because of a moment of Impulsiveness. You want to see pretty graphs of your progress. And you may want to make it public or put some money on it, knowing that the money will actually vanish if you fail.

And so there was Beeminder[42]. Beeminder is a web service which lets you set arbitrary process-based goals and then holds you to them with all the reasonableness and firmness of your best friend who wants to see you succeed but won't take any more of your crap. It's got great graphs which will please you when you're ahead, motivate you when you're behind, and share with you the fear of the death that your goal is about to die when it's time for you to be the uncomfortable hero of your story. You can adjust any goal, but the changes only take effect a week later, which is far enough away to keep you honest: you want to give up now, but you can't, and you don't want your future self to give up, so you just keep going.

I've used Beeminder to make sure I was walking an hour a day, developing Quantified Mind for three hours a week, and working on the Skritter iPhone app for sixty hours a week. Many use it to lose weight, to exercise, to drink less, to work more, to keep their inboxes clear, to waste less time surfing the web, and to quit smoking. Most

---

electronic mountain trap somewhere. So instead your paranoia might fixate on any twenty-six-year-old "meat-body" which L. Ron Hubbard's thetan might be inhabiting.

42. https://www.beeminder.com

goals are a matter of effort over time, and for those types of goals, if they're important enough to warrant thirty seconds of bookkeeping a day, you should use Beeminder.

When writing this book, I put most of its goals into Beeminder without commitment contracts, because I already know I never lose at any Beeminder goal. I had goals like "Talk to a Hundred People" (7.7 new people a week), "Read Twenty Books" (one every 4.55 days), "Learn 3,000 Chinese Word Writings" (33 a day), and so on. It's free at first, but then if you fail a particular goal, you have to pledge a commitment contract of $5 to retry it the first time, $10 the second time, $30 the third time, $90 the fourth time, and so on, tripling with each subsequent failure time. With "Write A Book" (1,000 words a day until the first draft was done) and "Go Skydiving" (do it before August 25), I emailed the Beeminder crew and had them start me at $7,290 instead of working my way up. Here's the graph from the writing goal, where I finished the first draft with six weeks to spare[43].

---

43. The first flat period is where I planned to let myself skip writing during wedding travel. The second is where I approached thirty thousand words, realized the book would be short and I was done except for the last chapter on results, and let it sit before editing.

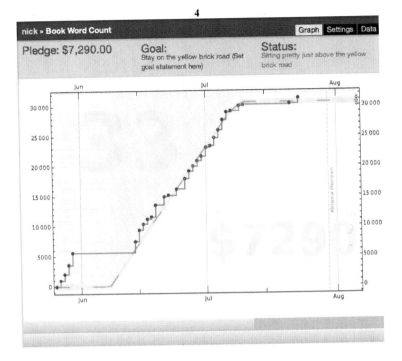

Pledge: $7,290.00   Goal: Status:
Stay on the yellow brick road (Set   Sitting pretty just above the yellow
goal statement here)   brick road

Read more and try it out at http://www.beeminder.com. It's almost always better than naive goal tracking methods[44] that only assess success or failure at the end, and it's free until you fail the second time. If you construct your success spiral well, though, you won't fail even once.

---

44. There's also http://stickK.com, which lets you do the commitment contracts with your friend as a referee. I prefer Beeminder in every way, but stickK does have better support for binary goals whether you try to do something every time (or never).

Burnt Ships

One specific technique for precommitment is where you disable, remove, or destroy a distraction or temptation. I call it "Burning the Ships" after the inaccurate story of Hernán Cortés who, after landing his invasion force, ordered his men to burn their ships[45] so that they wouldn't be distracted by the possibility of retreat when conquering the Aztec empire. You list possible distractions, and then you make it so that it's impossible to do those things when you want to be working toward your other goals. Then instead of having to use willpower to prevent yourself from going to go grab a snack, you realize that there are no snacks available, and you get on with your flow.

If Cortés were around today, he'd probably be one of us who turn our internet off. Apart from getting rid of your TV, that's usually what this technique comes down to, so maybe it should be called "Disconnecting the Internet." Startup maven Paul Graham has an excellent essay about the acceleration of addictiveness[46] in which he argues that to live a good life, one must become ever more eccentric in terms of saying no to the explosion of things that are designed to addict us, many of which are now delivered via the internet. Whether you're hooked on Facebook, email, news, your blog comments, cute kitten pictures, Words with Friends, YouTube, or even reading Wikipedia, it's harder to focus when a quick hit is right there on your computer or your phone. Do something about it, whether it's keeping your phone in airplane mode until 5pm, or turning off your laptop's WiFi at all times except 11:00 – 11:30 am and 8:00 – 9:00 pm. Or maybe it's even having a separate computer with no internet connection in your home office and going over there

---

45. Reinterpretation of the records show that he only ran aground most of the ships to thwart mutiny and left a few still available, so the history is a bad example. But the legend is a great example that everyone uses, which is why I still think of it this way.

46. http://paulgraham.com/addiction.html

to work. Even if you can resist these distractions while you're trying to focus, why would you want to have to?

"But I need internet to do my work!" If this is true, then you can set up browser extensions to block the sites that you don't want to visit during certain times, or whitelist the sites you do want to visit, or make a 30-second delay before your browser loads any page to stop that compulsive typing of reddit.com whenever you blank out for a second. But if this is just an excuse, if what you mean is that it's sometimes more convenient to be able to look things up, then turn it off anyway and look things up later. While writing this book, I needed to know who the guy with the burnt ships was. But for this book, I turned my internet off when going to bed, wrote during the mornings, and only turned it on again after lunch. So in the first draft, the guy was the famous general Really Alexander Hannibal. When editing, I then searched for every instance of the word "really" and did my research.[47]

This internetlessness was like a private beach for a man just let out of prison. I had tried various schemes to limit my email checking to no more than three times a day, or no more often than every 90 minutes, and to stop surfing over to skritter.com/forum whenever I had to wait 30 seconds for my code to compile. On good days, I managed it. Often, I weaseled. Sometimes I failed, checking dozens of times. At least I was no longer reading Hacker News (except when I did), never went on social networks except once at the end of the day to post iPhone app teaser bits for our users, and cleared my well-weeded blog feeds just twice a week. I was still working almost all the time. One week when I was gearing up to do 70 hours of real work (high for me, but not intense), I did a one-week timelapse of my screen[48], with my face in the corner, and showed it to some friends, figuring that it might be fun but that they would eventually skip through it. But every one of them watched the whole seven minutes and exclaimed to me afterwards how inspiring it was that I never checked Facebook!

---

47. Some writers put in placeholder text that is guaranteed not to be a word—I put in placeholders which are words I never want to use.
48. https://vimeo.com/39643329

I didn't think my focus was too great that week (so many emails checked and rechecked), but they were surprised by how good it was, and I was surprised by how low their standards were. Here I was, an internet addict, being praised because I was functioning. How bad are other people's addictions? I don't know, but if I was bad enough to need the internet turned off on me, then you can judge for yourself whether any reaction along the lines of "I don't need to turn it off" is good sense or defensive rationalization.

I started doing internetless mornings on the first day of writing this book. I also decided that I would only check email once per day, between Skritter work and dinner, and when I did check it, I would do all of it. It was easier than I thought, and far more effective. I could feel my brain jerk itself up from my writing, start bounding for the email, turn and try the Skritter forum, make as if to Google the phrasing of that gem-like flame quote, feint for the email again, and then, walled in on all sides by the knowledge that the internet was off, sit back down and continue writing, trying to pretend with dignity that it was just stretching. This tapered off over a week, and then my focus was always there: my writing speed went from a crawling 340 words per hour to a somewhat-less-slow 500, and I compressed my daily 130 incoming and 13 outgoing messages into an hour.

Why had this taken me so long to do? I had read countless times that I should eliminate distractions, and the first example was always to turn off the internet. (The second and third were usually to put on headphones and to set up a place to work where only work was allowed, and nothing else.) Maybe the answer is just that addiction is hard to admit. Or maybe it's easy, and there are other books, like this one except about addiction hacks instead of motivation hacks. I don't know where you get the spark to start, only how to fan it into an inferno once you have it.

Chapter Five: Social Skills

Get Ready For An Example

I want to give you an example of putting these motivation hacks (success spirals, precommitment, and burnt ships) into action all at once. Sometimes you'll face a goal which is so important it seems your life depends on it (high Value), but which seems so impossible (low Expectancy) that you'd rather die the slow death of escapism (high Impulsiveness) and ignore it until later (high Delay). You need all the motivation you can get, and you can't get any. It's so uncomfortable to think about your creeping doom that you develop an ugh field[49] around it, where your mind flinches away from thoughts about your goal. The ugh field spreads from your goal, to things related to your goal, to things that remind you of those things, and so on. Crushing debt is represented by bills, which come in envelopes, which are in your mailbox. Soon you can't even think about checking your mailbox without a shudder and a stiff drink.

When you're desperate, it's time to fight with every weapon you can. Your weapons, in this case, are not the Nerf Bat of Trying Harder or the Secret Wand of Easy Weight Loss. No. You'll wield the Sword of Last Chance. You'll make a plan to achieve your goal that requires time and effort, and you will carefully hack your motivation so that you'll put in said effort. If you have an ugh field surrounding your goal, it will be hard to admit that you need to do this. You might flinch away from the problem, saying to yourself, "I need to finish <Transparent Excuse> before I can focus on reducing my drinking," or "I could probably start dating any time, but I can wait until after this work project is done." I find that journaling helps with this. It's much easier for me to tell when I'm lying to myself when I write things down, or especially when I hesitate to write

---

49. http://lesswrong.com/lw/21b/ugh_fields/

about something. If it's not a problem, then why am I so reluctant to engage it and prove that?

The example I will now give is the most important, most rewarding goal I've ever achieved. I had to use success spirals, precommitment, burnt ships, and a new environment. I was missing something which I needed and thought I could never have. I made a desperate plan, followed it for years, and acquired that missing piece. Many take this particular thing for granted, and some struggle with it, but few were ever as bad off as I was. Life without it was a combination of shame, fear, despair, and years spent escaping into books and video games. I lacked social skills.

Social Zero

I was eighteen, and I had no ability to talk to people. Outside my immediate family, I had no friends my age any more—I'd lost them years ago after I couldn't muster the courage to ask them to hang out. When my parents took my brother and me to Taco Bell, I would cower behind my mother and beg her to order for me, because the thought of saying, "Eleven bean and cheese burritos, no onions or sauce, please," was so terrifying that I'd rather not eat my favorite food. (She wouldn't do it, but my brother would.) The telephone was scarier than the dentist's drill. I once went through an entire day of high school—bus, eight classes, lunch—and realized I hadn't said a single word. I spent the rest of my time watching movies, reading fantasy books, and playing EverQuest, a game in which I logged almost a year of play time over five years. I felt like the ugliest, lamest creature that ever had to lurch out of its cave. I had no hope.

My lack of confidence had metastasized from my social skills to everything else. I thought I sucked at writing, despite my teachers' praise. I thought each new class would be too hard, even though I'd never been challenged in school. I was sure I'd never be able to work a job involving people, talk to a girl, make friends, survive college, drive a car, play sports, travel, or enjoy anything outside of my own entertainment.

I had mastered the use of success spirals in reverse: my Expectancy was zero for everything except taking standardized tests and kicking ass as my EverQuest paladin Warp, whom I roleplayed as a cocksure maniac who thought he could do anything. And because I was so addicted to that entertainment, my Impulsiveness was maxed out: I would always choose escape over any other pursuit.

The Delay of consequences was high, since the soonest I'd need to talk to anyone would be almost a year away, when I would go off to college—and I dreaded this so much that I never thought about it, long ago having smothered it in an ugh field. So even though the Value of learning social skills would be incalculable—the difference between life in the world and undeath in my room—I had no motivation to try to save myself. I convinced myself that this was okay even as I wrote angsty poetry about being a "silent toad among songbirds" and a "rounded stone that never rolled," too afraid to cry out for a push.

Desperation

That senior spring semester, I got my push. Well, it was more of a light breeze—not enough to set me moving, but enough to blow away a little of my ugh field. I had taken a class called **Writer's Workshop** with Mr. Mahle in the fall, and as I had then run out of classes to take, he gave me an independent study based on journaling.

When you have private writing assignments like **Write to yourself about your life path: what do you know about where you are coming from and where you are going?**, it gets tough to keep pretending that your life isn't a disaster heading for a catastrophe. I had to admit my terror at the thought of always being that way, of going to college in nine months, of being forever alone but for frequent visits from Shame.

In a desperate moment, I decided that I would never change if I kept playing computer games, and that if I quit right then, maybe some miracle might occur and I would be able to try to perhaps attempt to learn how to live once I got to college. This became a mantra—"once I get to college'—because that would be my last chance. I dared to hope that I would someday get from "mute" to "shy" and even be able to order my own food. I didn't hope that I'd have real friends or anything impossible like that, but maybe society could find some use for me.

I would never have been able to quit if it weren't for writing awful poetry. It was the only thing that offered me emotions as powerful as those I'd gotten from EverQuest. And because I was such a slow writer, it took up enough time to wean myself off the game. (I spent the rest of the time reading this new site called Wikipedia, which was a better addiction for me.)

I kept journaling, writing about how once I got to college I was going to talk to people, how I was going to change, how I was going to face my fears as if my life depended on it (which it did). This journaling was a form of precommitment: nine months of telling myself that I would take action would force me to swallow those promises if I didn't follow through, and knowing that helped make me believe that I could do it. And while I couldn't bring myself to tell anyone else what I had planned for when I left, I did somehow tell my family that I was quitting EverQuest, which along with uninstalling the game helped me to stay away. I should have sold my character[50]—that would have been an even stronger burnt ship.

Confidence Man

When I arrived at Oberlin College that fall, I had just enough motivation to try talking to people. I almost couldn't do it, but because I had so firmly fixed that first week as my time to do or die[51], my Delay was small. I had a deadline. I knew that if I let the old Nick come here to this new place, he would never leave me. I didn't eat anything except Reese's cups for the first two days because I was

---

50. I probably could have gotten $2000 for him at the time, which would have been a profit of about $0.17 an hour.
51. Literally.

too afraid to ask anyone where the cafeteria was and how I could get food. (Turns out my dorm was the cafeteria dorm.)

But I managed a few attempts. One girl Leah gave me a laundry bag. My new roommate Josh told me stories about Portland. Another girl Lauren asked me how I was, and going for broke, I told her how I had never been able to talk to anyone before and how scared I was. I guessed that she would be weirded out and leave, but she offered me sympathy! Conversation! Warmth!

I could hardly believe it—everyone was *nice to me*. They invited me into their games. They waved me over to eat with them. They didn't mind my shyness or my lack of grace. It was all happening better than I had dreamt. I even started dating a girl that first semester.

This is not to say it was easy. I was still afraid with each new social thing that I tried to do, and I fled from many things for which I wasn't ready. But although I didn't know it, I was on a success spiral, and each new conversation fed my courage. I was so happy to be alive at last that I kept my social goals tiny. This allowed me to slowly grow the spiral without the risk of failure. If I had tried to learn social skills faster, then I would have failed at some point, fallen off my spiral, and lost faith in myself. It almost happened a couple times. Instead, I took it slow, and over the next eight years, I became ever better and more confident.

I'm not saying that I'm now the most social guy around, bristling with friends and throwing parties like confetti. That honor would be decided by a tough call between my twin brother Zach and my startup cofounder George. But I fearlessly danced like a moron at both of their weddings last week, and about twenty people at each complimented me on my speech, some telling me it was the greatest best man speech that they had heard.

Rejection Therapy

Learning social skills doesn't have to take eight years, even from scratch. I didn't know about motivation hacking when I stumbled into my plan, or I could have set myself up to try harder. And I could have done more effective practice than slowly warming up to whatever conversations and friendships happened to come my way. With any skill, you can come up with an exercise that will push you to just beyond your limits, where learning comes the fastest. And you already know how to use precommitment to get yourself to do the exercise. Here's an exercise that I did to help with talking to strangers and asking for things. It's called Rejection Therapy[52].

Most people feel reluctant to approach strangers and ask for things they want. The most classic example is the guy who is afraid to walk up to an attractive girl and start a conversation or get a phone number. You might be afraid to ask if you can join a game of frisbee, or if you can sit with some group at lunch, or if some guy would be willing to let you practice your Chinese with him. And even if you have no problem doing these things, there is a world of meaningful encounters which can be unlocked by making strange requests that cut through protective politeness patterns, whether with strangers or acquaintances or friends. Will you go on a vision quest with me? May I learn the art of collodion wet plate photography from you? Can I test drive your Subaru Impreza WRX STI Lancer Evolution Superduty GT Quad-Core Hemi Sport with the twin turbos and DTRLs? You don't get to play basketball with the President[53] or sell your own breakfast cereal[54] if you're not comfortable putting yourself out there and hustling.

Why should we fear rejection? We can guess at an evolutionary psychological explanation that when you lived in a tribe of 50 people, being rejected by one of the four eligible mates would mean losing a quarter of your dating pool, so it would make sense to be cautious and avoid possible rejection. But today's dating pool is much larger, and most of the strangers you could make a fool of yourself in front of will never see you again. There is no longer much need to fear rejection from strangers.

---

52. http://rejectiontherapy.com/
53. http://www.fourhourworkweek.com/blog/2012/04/04/playing-b-ball-with-obama-6-steps-to-crossing-anything-off-your-bucket-list/
54. http://www.avc.com/a_vc/2011/03/airbnb.html

Rejection Therapy is an exercise designed to get you over this useless fear. It uses the psychological tactic of "flooding": you expose yourself to the terrifying stimulus over and over until you get over it and instinctively realize there's nothing to be afraid of. There are a few different flavors, like the thirty-day challenge where you must be rejected at least once per day, but the one that I did only took an hour.

Some friends and I walked downtown together, joking nervously about what we were going to do. We agreed to meet again in an hour to recount the stories of our many rejections and then headed off alone in different directions. The mission was to approach as many strangers as possible and ask them for things which we actually wanted, which would likely be rejected, which left us in a vulnerable position instead of the other person, and which were not so implausible as to no longer be scary.

I had a time limit, a social expectation, and a precommitment to doing it, so I fought down my terror and started asking for things. "Can I take your picture?" "May I try on your hat?" "Will you tell me a secret?" "Can I have a free ice cream?" "Will you give me a tour of the library?" "Can you tell me about the economics of panhandling?" "Can I play that Pac Man for free?" "May I ride in the bookmobile?"

A surprising amount of people said yes. I got the ice cream. I didn't get the library tour or the bookmobile ride, but the librarian was summoned and he told me a ghost story about the library which he'd only shared with a few people. No one let me take their picture, but I have a picture of me trying on a crazy hat. I went from initially terrified to mostly chill by the end of the hour, and that desensitization has stuck with me ever since[55].

After the hour was up, I met up with my friends. One guy had gotten three hairs from people's heads to cast a spell to summon an artificial intelligence to battle the evil god Cthulhu. One girl had gotten a free bike lock and a ride on someone's bike. One guy failed

---

55. I recently tried to do a related exercise in a posh mall, but it seems like my Rejection Therapy courage had only strengthened over time. Nothing was scary any more: dancing poorly in public, singing, asking people to hold my feet while I do a handstand, sprinting up crowded escalators while crying, "Tornado!"—there was no more apprehension to overcome.

to get anyone to meditate with him, and another couldn't get anyone to give him a dollar. Another got to try on several people's shoes. One guy asked for and received a nice jacket, which we later priced at $150. Everyone had reaped years of confidence in an hour.

One friend pointed out another useful benefit of this exercise, which was that it made obvious what it felt like to be rationalizing (making excuses to yourself). When you make yourself the rule, *I'm going to ask the next person I see if I can have a hug*, and then you see someone who looks particularly terrifying to approach, your brain will try to help you out with some rationalizations: ... *except for her, since she's too pretty / too old / too young / walking with someone / going somewhere / too tall / too looking-like-she-doesn't-want-to-be-bothered*. This feeling, of wanting or not wanting to do something for a basic reason (fear, laziness, hunger, etc.) and then giving yourself a higher-level excuse for why that's okay, should trigger alarms whenever you notice it.

Note that this rationalization is also how most goals die—you convince yourself that it's okay to not do what you told yourself you would do—and if you can develop the habit of noticing it and defeating it, then you'll be more effective in achieving your goals. I fixed twenty unpleasant bugs that I'd been avoiding for months in the first three days after I started practicing the noticing of rationalization. (I later lost the habit, which is a tough one. Later I'll try another exercise to get myself to hold onto the skill of avoiding rationalization.)

More Exercises

Rejection Therapy is one example of an exercise that gives huge gains in a short time if you can bring yourself to do it. With the powers of precommitment, you can set yourself up to do many such exercises, building skills and getting over fears in no time.

Another such exercise is the eye contact exercise. Most of us don't make enough eye contact. I don't know if I buy the stories about how all you need to do is look people in the eyes and everyone will trust and like you, no one will be able to resist you or tell whether you're lying, and you'll be promoted to Chief Billionaire in six months. But it's plausible that life is better seen through eyes than shoes and horizons, so I practiced with some guy I hardly knew. We decided to look into each other's eyes for fifteen minutes, noting each time the other guy looked away. It was uncomfortable at first and I didn't want to do it, but it was enough for me to get over my discomfort and look into people's eyes from then on. This worked with the other people I knew who also tried it.

I was going to do the same exercise with hugs, where you would hug someone unfamiliar for fifteen minutes, but I missed the exercise and never rescheduled. Long hugs and bro hugs still discomfort me. Writing this makes it clear that I need to find a stranger and do the hug exercise. This is a scary thought, so I will use precommitment to bind myself to actually do it, while setting the date to be far enough in the future so that it's not so scary right now that I won't commit.

You could design similar exercises for any small skill that you need to acquire, or any large skill which can be broken down into smaller skills[56]. Lifehacker Luke Muehlhauser has broken down social skills into a map of such skills[57], from handshakes to reading faces to hairstyle, which you can look through to find techniques to learn or to see how you might apply the technique to other areas.

---

56. http://lesswrong.com/lw/5p6/how_and_why_to_granularize/
57. http://www.mindmeister.com/96422213/social-effectiveness-skills

As an example, you might break down front-crawl swimming into dozens of skills, from breathing into the water to having your hand enter the water without splash to rotating your body with each stroke. Then you could come up with a drill for each skill: stand in the pool and breathe in above water and out below water a bunch of times; stand there and push your arm smoothly into the water for five minutes; hold your breath for a few strokes while you focus only on making sure you rotate enough. So while learning the front crawl by trying to do the front crawl should seem too difficult, learning to do it by learning each subskill one-by-one should seem encouragingly easy if you break it down far enough.

With many skills and drills, it's good to get feedback on your technique, because you don't want to practice the wrong things in the wrong ways. This isn't an excuse not to practice; it doesn't take much coaching to get started.

Chapter Six: Time Coins

You Have to Choose

My favorite quote is "i luv this song its grate i rememebr whn i first hurd it when i was six a ran around the rfrontromm lol."[58]

My second-favorite quote comes from the poet Carl Sandburg: "Time is the coin of your life. It is the only coin you have, and only you can determine how it will be spent. Be careful, lest you let other people spend it for you."

When you hack your motivation, you grow rich in time coins—rich enough to buy almost any life you could want. This makes it even more important for you to decide what life you want. Most of us spend our time coins doing jobs that other people have given us to do, saving the rest for entertainments that other people are trying to sell us.

Why do we not destine greater roles for ourselves? Why aren't we lion tamers, astronauts, champion martial artists, powerful rappers, or international spies? Why don't we make our own magician's magazines, brew up beatboxing bacteria, race rally cars, or shoot explosive arrows? A few of us do these things, but what is keeping the rest of us from the most fulfilling, exciting, Value-filled lives we can imagine?

If you're like most of us, the answer is some mix of "I can't do that," "I have to do this instead," and "I never thought of it, and now it's too late." Some of these excuses are true. You aren't going to play pro basketball if you're 5'3"[59]. You'll have to pay off most of your debt before you can start your own business. If you have tiny children, don't run off on your own to the Shaolin Temple to master

---

58. YouTube user evoguy1620 commenting on Run-D.M.C.'s "It's Like That"
59. This is a lie. Muggsy Bogues was a successful NBA player at 5'3", which goes to show that even the classic examples people use when they tell you that you can't do something are not entirely true.

kung fu. (Bring them.) But most of these excuses are rationalizations borne from low Expectancy.

If you aren't good at something yet, then hack your motivation to spend the time practicing, and you'll become great[60]. If you need to work a job to survive, then motivate yourself to hack at your goal outside of work, save money, or find a better job. If you don't know how to do something, then motivate yourself to spend the time figuring it out. Many stories are told of ordinary, unfulfilled folks who, late in life, suddenly challenged themselves and changed everything to realize their dreams. Many more such stories are never told, because their protagonists never protagonized. Effort can solidify almost any dream, and motivation hacks can ensure effort.

With so many goals in front of you, how do you choose? You don't want to end up as a mistaken entrepreneur who should have been a dancer just because you read a book which lent you its author's dream in place of your own.

Spending time coins without a plan is expensive, but at least you have feedback mechanisms like boredom, stress, and depression to tell you when you're living your life wrong. When you hack motivation, you sever those nerves. You'll need to instead rely on high-level planning and introspection to figure out what you should be doing. I was presenting a time-graphing design for making work more rewarding, and one guy objected that he had been a programmer, and it had eventually become frustrating enough that he quit and changed industries, and if he had artificially made it more fun to work as a programmer, then he never would have been forced into a better career. My friend Divia answered better than I could, "Pain and pleasure indicators cannot take the place of being strategic about one's goals."

So even though this is a book about motivation and not goals, I would feel cruel without writing a chapter on making sure you know what you want before making sure that you're going to get it.

---

60. If you practice deliberately, that is: focusing on strengthening your weaknesses efficiently, not just doing more of what you're already good at.

Goal Picking Exercises

Sometimes it seems as if there are more exercises for choosing your goals than there are goals worth choosing. This is okay. Pick your favorite exercises and do them. I'll offer three good ones that you can use.

1. Imagine your ideal day. What do you do? Whom do you talk to? Where do you go? Then pick a few goals that will bring your days closer to this ideal.

2. Make a list of every crazy goal you can think of. Then rate each goal on three factors: how much the goal excites you, from one to ten; your probability of success if you tried as hard as you could; and how long it would take in hours[61]. Then sort the goals by excitement times probability of success divided by time required and pick some of the most efficient goals.

3. Imagine that you're another person, more competent than yourself, who was just dropped into your current life at this moment, without any of your current obligations but with all of your current predicaments. Forget everything that has come before and where you used to be going. What would you do? This is an exercise in overcoming the Sunk Cost Fallacy[62].

I did all three of these for this book project, with a three-month limit. I imagined an ideal day for myself: waking up at the crack of dawn, getting exercise and early sun before anyone was up, reading and studying Chinese in a park, waking Chloe up for breakfast, and so on.

I made a spreadsheet of a ton of cool goals I could do in three months, and realized I had time for all of them if I cut out hang gliding and dancing (too much time) as well as learning the guitar

---

61. Convert any monetary costs to equivalent time costs for how long it would take to make that money.
62. The more you invest in something, the harder it becomes to abandon it, even when it no longer makes sense, like when I finish any Lars von Trier film.

(not exciting enough). I hadn't thought of learning skateboarding, knife throwing, or lucid dreaming before, but once brainstormed, those goals kept striking me, and I knew they wouldn't take long.

I started the whole project by taking the outside view of my situation and asking, "Would a protagonist keep striving desperately on his startup even after desperation gave way to prosperity?" No— he would strive to ignite all the freedom he had earned.

When you do pick your goals, forget the advice about SMART goals.[63] Use Piers Steel's slightly improved CSI Approach. Your goals should be Challenging (if they're not exciting, they won't provide Value); Specific (abstract goals can leave you vulnerable to Impulsiveness, since it's not clear what you need to do); Immediate (avoid long-Delayed goals in favor of ones you can start now and finish soon), and Approach-oriented. (As opposed to avoidance goals, where you try not to do something, you should instead reframe it positively as an attempt to do something—it just feels better.) I talk more about this in Chapter 12: *Mistakes*.

Bad Ways to Dream

There are many bad ways to pick your goals. Watch out for them, don't use them in the future, and re-examine any current goals that came from them.

A terrible way to pick your goals is to do what society wants you to do: to chase prestige. Don't do things to win the respect of people you don't know. Instead, do things that you and people whom *you* respect care about. Paul Graham puts it best: "Prestige is just fossilized inspiration. If you do anything well enough, you'll *make* it prestigious."[64]

---

63. There are many forms of this acronym since its invention for team planning in the 1980s, like: Specific, Measurable, Attainable, Relevant, and Time-bound. These are redundant: if something is measurable and time-bound, it's specific.

There's also the SMARTER variant, where they add Evaluation (scheduling reflection on how your goal is going) and Revision (adjusting the goal based on the evaluation). That's getting away from formulating goals and into how you do them, but it's a good addition.

64. Read Paul Graham's excellent essay, "How to Do What You Love" at

Paul also tells a cautionary tale about his friend who knew when she was in high school that she wanted to be a doctor. She was so motivated that she persevered through every obstacle, including not actually liking her work. She's a successful doctor, and she hates it. Now she has a life chosen for her by a high-school kid.

This is another source of bad goals: childhood dreams. Some childhood dreams are originally ours, and some grow on us, but most were given to us at a time when we didn't know any better about what we liked. If what you're clutching is no longer a dream but a memory of one, then drop it.

Bad goals often take the form of intermediate steps. You might want to be rich. If so, then go do something that will make a lot of money—don't go to college, fight your way out of debt, work your way up, and then be rich. That's safety, not wealth. And if you want to play in a band or sail around the world or write novels, then don't make money first. You'll have lost your passion by the time you look for it. Sometimes there are no exciting paths to an exciting goal: you can't be a doctor without years of schooling. But do you want to be a doctor, or do you want to heal people? Gatekeepers will tell you that you need to crawl before you can walk before you can be certified to begin. Run past them.

Watch out for things that you have always been good at. It always seems to make sense to keep doing them, to build on your previous accomplishments, and to play to your strengths. This can lead to greatness, but it can also be a trap. I had always been good in school, and so I kept taking classes in all of my best subjects. Before I knew it, I graduated with 142 out of 112 credits, highest honors, a triple major in Computer Science, Applied Mathematics, and East Asian Studies, and only two close friends (my startup cofounders). My college adventure count was low, and I never used my high GPA[65], my degree, or anything I learned in those extra classes I slept through.[66] That was dumb. The only thing it's good for is impressing

---

http://www.paulgraham.com/love.html
65. I just had to send a letter to my college to figure out what my GPA was, never mind remembering how many credits I had.
66. I always learned more doing things outside of class, apart from Chinese class, which is the only one I could stay awake in.

people I don't know, so I try not to bring it up except in warnings not to play others' games. I hope you are not impressed.

Goals that are too easy are goals that won't excite you. There is not enough Value in "lose five pounds" to make you care. It's too safe. It's probably easier for the overweight motivation hacker to lose fifty pounds than fifteen, because he'll know he needs to try harder, and he'll want it more. The daily process of achieving the goal is the same, but it takes longer and gives him more Value. It's not even a real increase in Delay, since he is rewarded throughout the process and not just at the end. A sure way to kill motivation is to water down the challenge. This seems as if it contradicts Expectancy and the idea of success spirals, where you make sure you can't lose, but the key is to set your success spirals around the process ("I Expect that I can use Beeminder to make sure I lift weights twice a week") while deriving your Value from the results ("I'm getting stronger, and one day I'll deadlift 500 pounds!"). You can't quite guarantee that effort will lead to success, but you can guarantee effort, and that almost always leads to success eventually if you just don't quit.

The biggest source of goals, both good and bad, is stories of what other people have done. If you read enough about startups, you'll want to do one, perhaps forgetting that you value financial security. If your friends all start running, you may find yourself running with them, even though you actually hate it. Growing up watching romantic comedies will give you horrible ideas about what you want from a lover. Go ahead and travel the world, but pay attention to whether you enjoy it. Then there are the other types of stories: not of action and adventure, but of common contentment. Most people you know work jobs, buy things, go out, entertain themselves, and eventually start families. These may not be necessary goals for you. "Moderation in all things," they say. That may keep a society together, but it's not the protagonist's job.

On Happiness

Humans don't know what makes us happy. We think we know, but we're usually wrong. Psychologist Daniel Kahneman draws a distinction between the experiencing self and the remembering self[67]. We have two modes of thinking about well-being: the experiencing self, which can semi-accurately tell you how happy you are in the moment if you ask yourself, and the remembering self, which can make up reasonable-sounding lies about how happy you were in the past, or about how happy something will make you in the future.

Life is made up of a series of moments. The happiness and unhappiness within a life is integral—the area under the curve—of the happiness of those moments. Only a tiny fraction of a life is experienced in a reflective mode (since we don't spend much time consuming memories). In other words, the well-being described by the remembering self is an illusion.[68] You could call the well-being given by the experiencing self "happiness" and that given by the remembering self "life satisfaction".

Unfortunately for us, the remembering self makes all the planning decisions, charting all of our goals across its bizarre cognitive geography. We ignore process and focus on conclusion; we overestimate both negative and positive impacts of possible events; we hyperbolically discount like a fishmonger going out of business; and we make disconnected events fit into consistent life stories. We end up with bad goals that don't make us happy while we're achieving them and which give only fleeting satisfaction when we're done. Almost all attempts to increase our happiness end in failure because we don't understand what actually makes us happy. And when you set yourself up to accomplish a goal no matter how unpleasant the process is, that's not a recipe for well-being.

I say again: it is dangerous to hack motivation with the wrong goals. Whenever you override instincts with higher cognitive processes, you'd better do it well, because otherwise you'll hurt

---

67. http://www.ted.com/talks/daniel_kahneman_the_riddle_of_experience_
vs_memory.html
68. Some disagree with me on how much this life satisfaction is worth. Watch the
TED talk from the previous video and decide for yourself.

yourself. It's like lifting weights: if you don't learn proper form, an injury will leave you weaker than if you hadn't even tried.

My solution to calibrating my remembering self's planning to my experiencing self's well-being is to randomly ping myself to record my happiness *right now*, along with what I'm doing. A timestamped alert comes in on my phone or laptop about every three hours, and I type in a 1-10 happiness number[69] and a couple tags for whatever is making me feel good or bad. An example entry might be: "2012-06-12 Tue 03:17   7: music, iPhone app launch". There are many ways to measure experiential happiness, so find what works for you. You might be able to just develop a habit of mentally interrupting yourself to ask how you're doing and why. But if you're human, don't neglect this. Humans don't know what makes us happy, so measure[70].

I agreed to go whitewater rafting, thinking, "Outdoor action adventure! This is going to be a lot of fun." When the day came, though, I remembered to sample my experiential happiness throughout the trip—not using my phone, but with constant attention. Here's the breakdown:

• Two uncomfortable hours in the car on the way there at a happiness level of 4 / 10.

• An hour waiting to start at a neutral 5.

• An hour of rafting at 6.

• Short bursts of 8 when we went through rapids.

• Another hour of 4 as I developed a headache from eating only the terrible sandwiches the guides brought for lunch.

• The last headache-hour of the rafting at 5 with brief 8s.

• Two starved and nauseous hours at 3 on the way home.

• A one-hour 5 dinner where we'd all run out of things to say.

---

69. This is on a logarithmic scale where each point above five doubles happiness, and each point below five doubles unhappiness.

70. There is a caveat here that if you tend to focus on happiness and get disappointed when you're not happy, then you may suffer more from the occasional unhappiness. I find that curiosity (expressed in the tracking process itself) is a better response than extra disappointment.
http://www.psychologytoday.com/blog/intense-emotions-and-strong-feelings/201207/just-being-happy-can-be-complicated

Average experiential happiness for those nine hours: 4.47. My average happiness was 6.18 for the month before that, mostly from sitting at home listening to music and writing code. Bad planning, remembering self! And if I hadn't measured it, my remembering self would probably have told me, just days later, that yeah it was a long car ride but what a blast those rapids were! Watch out for low fun density.

My two years of happiness tracking has surprised me[71]. I thought sunny weather was crucial for me and wanted to move from Pittsburgh to California. Nope; weather was only 3% of happiness and 1% of unhappiness. (I moved to California anyway, but for the people, not the weather.) My happiness from music used to be 14%, and I hadn't taken any time to manage what music I listened to. When I found that out, I spent two days organizing my music collection to cull the bad stuff, increasing the density of enjoyable songs and bringing that up to 22%, increasing my overall positive happiness by 10%. Not bad for two days of effort.

Now, almost all my happiness comes from enjoyable work (25%), music (22%), and feeling accomplished (10%)[72]. My unhappiness (which is about half as large as my happiness) is split between work (18%), lack of accomplishment (16%), tiredness (12%), and physical discomfort (12%). This is after improving previous problem areas like others' negativity and reading Hacker News and other internet media.

But I noticed some low-overhead, high-Value activities in there that I rarely did: reading books, writing, reading, pyromania, playing short rounds of video games with friends, and photography. Looking at these activities, I already had a good idea of how I should fill my days during this project. I had been having a lot of fun lately just working and listening to music, but I wanted to do better than that. I measured my average happiness for the three months before I started this book: 6.3 / 10, the highest it had ever been. I decided that the

---

71. I wrote some code to do a linear regression on the tags, then made a pie chart in Excel. It's not rigorous, but it's the most helpful self-tracking I've done.
72. That 10% of happiness from accomplishment and the 16% of unhappiness from lack of it represent all the weight that I should place on life satisfaction.

next three months should double my happiness, raising it whole point to 7.3 / 10.

To hit a 7 on my scale, I have to visibly look happy: smiling, rocking my head to music, or staring determined at my work with fire in my eyes. I knew that I'd need goals that kept me burning all day to pull it off. The goals you choose should do the same: they should drench you in Value and then ignite you.

Chapter Seven: Startup Man

A Lifetime of Work

Paul Graham once wrote that doing a startup is "a way to compress your whole working life into a few years."[73] Working on your own startup can provide more motivation than anything else I know. You do those forty years of work in four years not just because you have to, but also because it's fun. This chapter uses the story of my startup Skritter as a study in motivation. You don't have to have a startup to see how you might apply a startup-style combination of high Expectancy, high Value, low Impulsiveness, and low Delay to transform your motivation environment.

For me, the best thing about doing a startup wasn't the financial freedom I achieved, but the lesson in how it feels to love what you're doing. After finishing that first ¾ lifetime[74] of work, I'm aiming to work at least a few more lifetimes. It's more fun than simply having fun.

An Idea That Doesn't Suck

It was 4 A.M. in Beijing, and I awoke in my friend's Chinese dorm room with a cold, near-deafness from my flight, and total confusion as to where I was. I had just returned from three weeks of hearts-and-rainbows volunteering at an NGO[75] in Chongqing with innocent Chinese college girls to spend two days with some rowdy American students, and I had a massive case of reverse culture shock. When I got to Beijing, I met them at a restaurant where they'd spent the last eleven hours drinking, eating pizza, and playing cards

---

73. http://paulgraham.com/wealth.html
74. Doing a bootstrapped startup is not as stressful as doing a funded startup because risk and reward are more balanced. You work just as hard, but you live longer.
75. NGO: Non-Governmental Organization. This one was promoting HIV/AIDS awareness.

with the mohawked owner. They were so drunk that I won twenty consecutive rounds of a card game to which I didn't know the rules. Because my ears felt as if they were fifteen feet away from my head, my waking life felt more surreal than the dream I had just come from, and that was before I saw Nick Hatt.

Hatt had also come to China that winter term of junior year from Oberlin College (to research the Beijing underground rap scene, not to volunteer at an NGO); was also a Computer Science and East Asian Studies major; was also named Nick; and was also staying in my childhood friend Clark's dorm room. I thought I was hallucinating when I saw him, since he had no affiliation with Clark and there are a lot of dorm rooms in Beijing.

Realizing that we had the same 7:30 am flight out from Beijing did not help convince me of my lucidity, nor did the plan to hit a Chinese McDonald's at 4:30 am beforehand. I had gotten three hours of sleep that night, but Hatt had apparently stayed up, chugging water and playing his Nintendo DS to stay awake. My surreality dial broke off at 11 when I asked him what he was playing. "It's this game where you're a ninja surgeon and you have to perform surgery in combat while other ninjas try to kill you. Each incision flashes onto the screen, and you have to react quickly to trace the stroke and cut the patient open," he responded not-in-Chinese from far away.

I could not process this. I think I just moaned at him. But in that moment, he gave me an idea which would go on to win me financial freedom.

To learn Chinese well, one must learn thousands of Chinese characters, ranging from as simple as the one-stroke character 一 (yī: "one") to more complicated than the 36-stroke 齉 (nàng: "snuffle"). Students of Chinese build mountains of flashcards for these characters, which eventually fall over and crush the students. Some students survive, giving up the idea of learning to write and instead crawling to shaky, reading-only literacy after a thousand hours of study. After three exhausting semesters of Chinese, my writing was already collapsing, so when I saw Hatt scratching out those surgical strokes on his screen, I thought, "Wouldn't it be great if I could learn the strokes of Chinese characters with some stroke-based handwriting recognition game?"

I came home, told the story a few times, and forgot about the idea for a few months, until I needed a senior Computer Science honors project topic. I was babbling to my friend Ben about some ant colony optimization algorithm visualization when he said, "No, that's stupid. What about that Chinese writing algorithm you were talking about?"

I sputtered for a few moments about how that wouldn't... I mean, it might not... well, I suppose I could, but... hmm. Ben stared at me until I admitted, "That's not such a bad idea."

I had been reading all these posts on Hacker News about how one should do a startup instead of getting a job, and my roommate George had previously agreed to do a startup with me if I could find an idea that didn't suck and if I would stop bothering him because he had to do his economics homework. I convinced him and my other roommate Scott that the idea didn't suck, I skipped half of my math classes to hack on the stroke recognition algorithms, we won $30,000 from the college's Creativity & Leadership fund to get started, we found a cheap apartment in town, and we were off as soon as we graduated.

Overnight, we went from working as little as we had to for school, to as much as we could for ourselves. We ran into setbacks, fought terrible bugs, designed bad interfaces, fundraised in uncomfortable shoes, lost almost all our users when we started charging, incinerated cash in Google AdWords, rewrote everything again and again, built features that didn't matter, marketed ineffectively, and spent a wrist-searing January with thirty-one cloudy days typing in Chinese-English dictionary entries, assembling thousands of characters stroke by stroke, and hunching over a stroke-classification tool I built called "The Drudge." But we loved it, and without a schedule or any deadlines, we found ourselves doing fifty hours of Real Work a week. Why? What was it about the startup that gave us so much motivation?

Motivation Extravaganza

I'll break down our startup experience into factors affecting the four terms of the motivation equation. These factors will suggest more general techniques that you can use in shaping your own motivation environment.

Expectancy

We were committed. We committed to at least a year for the $30K grant, we didn't have any other fallbacks, and we told everyone we were doing it. With your goals, do the same: don't leave yourself any safe ways to fail, and you'll be more confident of success.

We focused our expectancy on the process, not the result. Startup success is a gamble, which does detract from expectancy. But we'd read Paul Graham's advice for startups: just don't die, and you'll succeed eventually. He was right in our case. If you never give up, you'll make it, even if you have to try many different approaches. We didn't know whether our startup would make money, but we did know we would work hard and not disgrace our families. Many goals are similar: don't worry about winning, just ensure that you'll keep going.

We were overconfident. First-time startup founders underestimate the difficulty of creating something great. Everyone said it would be hard, but luckily for us, we couldn't understand them. "We'll pitch the investors with twenty million in revenue after three years. Silly investors! We'll only be making four million by then." Mm-hmm. Goals won't always trick you this way, but when they do, be grateful: you are capable of more than you know[76], so the larger the challenge, the better.

We had cofounders. I would never have gotten through some of the bug mountains if Scott hadn't been there digging next to me. George would have gotten a part-time job and/or killed himself if I

---

76. Mom says, "When you're a beginning baby writer, you have to think that you're writing the most awesome stuff... But it's so necessary, because if you understood the magnitude of your incompitude, you'd just die."

hadn't balanced his revenue-projection pessimism with my optimism. Scott would have burnt out if George wasn't the funnest guy on the planet. When you hit a low by yourself, it's hard to get out of it. When your bros just keep going, you'll stumble after them even if you've lost the light, only to find that it was just ahead at the next bend. Don't strive alone if you don't have to.[77]

Value

We chose the most important thing we'd ever done. There was a direct connection between our work each day and the lifetime of freedom we'd win if we succeeded. Pick goals that matter to you.

We worked for ourselves. In a three-person startup, you do only tasks that you decide need doing because you want them done or because you want to help out your best friends. Writing a twenty-page FAQ is easier than writing a bogus two-page paper on the feminine gaze in *Hiroshima mon amour*. Do your own thing, not someone else's.

We worked for our users. We made it so easy for users to contact us that thousands of them did, many to tell us how much they loved Skritter. When I had "It's a truly amazing, amazing site!" and "Your site's signup page is down" in my inbox, I hungered to work. When I was building a huge new feature that no one was trying yet, that was when I struggled with motivation. (This is part of why they say you should launch early.) Find a way to get people counting on you and appreciating your struggle.

We picked a fun startup to build. Skritter is almost like a game, and we got to do a lot of fun things with it—even put in a few explosions here and there. Fun is part of value! It's much easier to make money building maximally unsexy products like inventory management software because there's less competition for boring work, but we wanted to make something cool, even if it was less profitable. (And indeed, we made almost nothing for the first two years. That part sucked.) You might be more motivated by

---

77. If you feel alone, join a group with which to share your struggles and successes, either online or offline. There are many people out there with the same goals, and they're waiting to connect with you.

mountains of cash than we were, but don't overlook the fun factor. Enjoying something is part of doing it well.

We picked a fun way to build it. We worked from home, and our headquarters was our guest bedroom. We got to work closely together, listen to music, eat lunch on the porch, and play games and blow things up after dinner. This was so much fun that we wanted to keep the startup going just so that we could keep hanging out. Merge your goals into the lifestyle that you want to lead.

We had enough energy. We slept as much as we wanted, since there was no schedule. We got exercise, avoided processed food, and ate healthy dinners that Scott cooked for us. We did eat cereal for breakfast and succumbed to the simplicity of pasta when there weren't enough leftovers, so sometimes we did get tired in the afternoons, but we'd just go for a walk around the neighborhood when that happened. Everything is more fun when you're awake. To ensure focus, optimize your energy levels.

We shielded each other from terrible tasks. Now, with just three guys, we each still had to do almost everything, including many unpleasant, value-less tasks, some of which I listed earlier. Scott and I hated business paperwork and would sooner flee the country than get our lawyer to sign the amended articles of incorporation. George disliked it less, so he took care of it. He hated using Facebook and Twitter to manage our social media presence, so I did that frustrating chore. Scott minded accounting less, so he accounted, and he cooked, saving George and I from endless repeats of "The Bean Dish." Each of us was more willing to take his bullets when he saw the others doing the same. I use this technique all the time with Chloe, too: "I'll do the laundry; what will you trade me? Dinner? Deal[78]!" Unlike with money, we all have different preferences for chores, so trade tasks with someone and you can both get great deals.

Impulsiveness

---

78. More common trades would be me listening to the Jason Mraz album and her cuddling my head seven times, or me going to see *Wicked* and her cooking three dinners for me.

We created a work environment that afforded only work. This sounds like the opposite of working from home, but in our case, we had always worked from that home, so it was an easy habit—wake up, start working. I did have to put a rubber duck on my right speaker to signal George when not to ask me what I thought about buying some katanas or how many Twizzlers a bear could eat, but that was a solvable problem. One advisor told us that we should get an office, because that's where you're supposed to work. "You won't get distracted in an office, so you'll be more productive." Poor guy— avoiding distractions doesn't mean driving twenty minutes away and renting space where there's nothing fun to do. Find or create a new environment and use it only for work, even if it's just for set times of day. Leave bad habits at your new door, and they'll stay out.

We didn't have much else to do. We were in a college town of 8,000 people, and most of our friends had graduated. It's not usually a good thing to have nothing in life but work, but it did help us focus. (Later, when we moved the startup to Costa Rica, our focus was no match for the jungles and rivers and mountains and surfing and *ticos*[79], so we didn't get much done.) Apple cofounder Steve Jobs said that you should stay hungry[80] in order to do great things. If your life is full, you won't have the same drive as a desperate man. This doesn't matter for many goals, but watch out if you're trying to compete with those hungry desperados—they want it more than you do, so you'll have to be extra smart about structuring your motivation in order to work as hard as they will.

We were around people who were working. (Each other.) We didn't have a schedule or any rules about how much to work. We could each just read a book in the middle of the day if we wanted. But when you've got a guy in the same room soldiering on for your shared destiny, then it doesn't feel right to slack off. This was actually a problem for George, because as the designer he often got way ahead of us developers[81] and would run out of work to do,

---

79. Costa Ricans informally call themselves *ticos*. By the end of our trip, our friend Gumercindo, who had initially pegged us as *gringos*, apologized and welcomed us as *ticos* ourselves.
80. http://news.stanford.edu/news/2005/june15/jobs-061505.html
81. The designer decides how something should be built and the developer builds it.

especially when we weren't fundraising. He'd see me there at night striving to code up an interface he'd mocked up, and his *Top Gear* episode would blur with tears of frustration at not being able to work more. Surround yourself with motivated people.

We played hard. After dinner, we'd usually go and play Super Smash Brothers for forty minutes, which I measured as one of the most fun things I can do as long as I don't overdo it. George had a built-in Smash guilt timer, and when it went off he'd stop playing, so we were forced to keep it short and fun-dense. On nights when we didn't Smash, we'd go off and read interesting articles on Hacker News for a couple hours and not feel half as charged up afterwards. If Scott and I had gotten too much better at Smash than George, he would have quit playing and Skritter would have died. Fortunately, we found some other fun things to do: Metalocalypse, thermite, an illegal laser, Guitar Hero, steel wool spark showers, a bad-ass knife, Worms, short films, a giant Fresnel lens, dry ice, street art, and quoting *Wizard People, Dear Reader* at each other instead of speaking English[82]. Because we knew we were going to max out on fun together after dinner, why would we waste work time playing a mildly fun tower defense game? Collect fun-dense[83] activities, then do those instead of spending more time on wimpy leisure distractions.

Delay

We always thought we were almost there. On the surface, the delay inherent in a startup seems motivation-killingly high. It can be years—or never—before you start making the money you could make tomorrow in a normal job. But unlike with fixed-duration goals like medical school, success never feels years away. When we started, we thought we'd launch in six months (it took twelve) and either be rich or broke in two years (it took four). We thought every new feature would catapult us into prosperity (only one of hundreds did:

Building takes much longer.
82. Yes, we developed an impenetrable subculture. Our girlfriends couldn't understand us, either, when they came to visit.
83. Fun density isn't obvious, so pay attention to how much fun you're having *while* you're having it.

auto-renewing credit card subscriptions), that each trade conference would spread our name throughout the land (not yet), that each marketing campaign would double our traffic (nope), and that each interface redesign would solve all our problems (it took six iterations before new users could make a vocabulary list more than half the time). Everyone thinks this way, and it's called the planning fallacy[84]. I think it's great: everything takes longer than we think, but if we planned accurately, we'd give up right away. When you're always almost done, the delay before your reward seems short, and so your motivation is high. You don't have to do anything to take advantage of this; even recognizing that it always takes longer won't save you from underestimating.

We released early and often. Every time we improved something, we couldn't wait to show it to our users—and so we didn't wait. We uploaded it to the site right away. This caused a lot of bugs, but it was way more fun than monthly releases and extensive quality assurance testing. One day I decided that I would translate the entire handwriting recognition algorithm from server-side Python to client-side ActionScript 3. Excited by the thought of stroke recognition being instant, and wanting to surprise Scott, George, and the users, I hacked for ten hours straight, using my epic motivation to write 1,000 lines of mathematically complex code that worked without logic errors the first time I ran it. (Usually I'm lucky to write ten lines without a mistake.) It was live the next morning when everyone woke up to hail me as a hero. I didn't give myself a deadline but a challenge, and the thought of immediate glory made me work far better than normal. For motivational highs, kill delay: look for ways to do something amazing right away.

iPhone App

After two-and-a-half years, we escaped the too-cozy bubble of Oberlin, Ohio and took the startup to Costa Rica for ten weeks in preparation for going remote so that George and I could be with our

84. http://lesswrong.com/lw/jg/planning_fallacy/

girlfriends and Scott could travel the world. As we left that motivation-rich work environment, we immediately dropped down to 24 hours a week, and even that was a struggle.

In Costa Rica lurked adventure and uncomfortable chairs. Then Pittsburgh, where Chloe was in grad school, held new friends, puzzle hunts, and rock climbing. She and I spent a summer in Silicon Valley, and with all the Less Wrong rationalists[85], Quantified Self lifehackers, and Hacker Dojo[86] entrepreneurs competing for my fascination, Skritter work was stalled at the 21 hours a week needed to fix bugs, answer email, and sputter meaninglessly on the Skritter iPhone app.

I wanted desperately to finish the app, but I couldn't make myself do the work. I had more bugs than ever, I was discouraged about my low work output, I was no longer hungry, I didn't have my bros at my side, I had everything instead of nothing else to do, and I could see that the iPhone app was many months away. Expectancy and Value were low, Impulsiveness and Delay were high, and my motivation was gone.

By this time, I'd learned about the motivation equation and realized that I needed to consciously design a motivating environment if I hoped to reach my goal (and have any fun doing it). I was like an athlete relearning how to move after an injury. I had lucked into a great motivation environment before, but now I needed to put one together from scratch.

To increase my Expectancy, I started a success spiral on my weekly iPhone app development hours, starting low at first so I knew I could do it, and putting it on Beeminder so I knew I would do it. The Value of finishing the app was already high, but the Value of working on it was low—fixing bugs sucked, and no one was using it yet and encouraging me. I decided to ignore the bugs for now and scramble on building the features I'd need to start alpha testing, since

---

[85] Less Wrongers like to hold meetups where people hang out and try to change their minds. Then some of them go into the naked hot tub. The first part is fascinating.

[86] The Hacker Dojo is a hackerspace: a warehouse full of eccentric people making anything from iPhone apps to fire-breathing bicycles. Sounds exciting, and in a way it is, but in another way it's usually just a bunch of people quietly typing on MacBooks, like a giant coffee shop with bad furniture and no food.

I'd like fixing bugs more when I had users to fix them for. This helped decrease my perceived Delay, since it was no longer months until finishing the app, but weeks until hitting alpha (it turned out to be months for alpha and almost another year until launch, but luckily I underestimated). And to limit Impulsiveness, I started using timeboxing[87] (allowing only a set, short time to work on something) for my email, waking up early and doing app development first while I wouldn't be distracted, and trying to cut back on the other things I was pursuing until only the coolest remained.

Of everything I did, using Beeminder to precommit, to build my success spiral, and to visualize my progresss was the most helpful. When I got back to Pittsburgh after that summer in California, I had managed to increase my daily iPhone development hours from 1.3 to 2.7 during the preceding month—still mostly doing website maintenance, but enough to show me that I could do more on the app. I cranked that Beeminder up to five hours a day of iPhone app development and held on for my life.

For the first three months, I skated the edge of death, never more than a day's work away from failing my Beeminder goal. But progress came, and my Expectancy grew stronger along with it. We launched our alpha version, and users loved it. We bought Scott a MacBook and brought him in on the iPhone app, too. Value went up, since he could do some of the parts I didn't want to, and I had more fun working together than on my own, even though it was remote. Delay decreased as we got closer to launch, although we continued to underestimate the remaining work. I became better and better at saying no to activities that had a low fun density, and as Chloe became busier finishing her master's and my other housemates learned that I was a badass samurai of work on a quest of ferocious focus, distractions diminished. After recharging with a five-friend, two-week trip to Mexico and Guatemala in January, motivation was bursting out of me. I soared over my Beeminder target of five hours a day.

---

87. The best reference for timeboxing starts here:
   http://www.alljapaneseallthetime.com/blog/timeboxing-trilogy-part-1-what-and-why

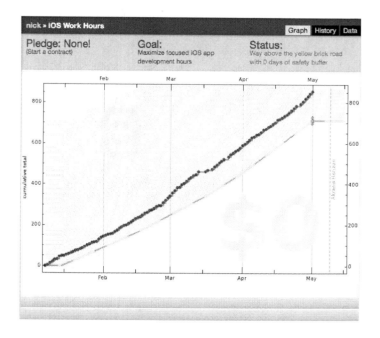

Pledge: None!
(Start a contract)

Goal:
Maximize focused iOS app
development hours

Status:
Way above the yellow brick road
with 0 days of safety buffer

At this point, I was having so much fun with the app that my
goal had changed from "work enough" to "work as much as
possible." My average happiness climbed to 6.3, the highest I had
ever sustained; burnout was not a concern. Beeminder was no longer
exerting any pressure, since I didn't need it any more, even after
increasing the goal rate a couple times. I switched to a method of
graphing my work time devised by psychologist Seth Roberts, which
he called percentile feedback[88]. The idea is that you graph your
progress throughout the day as a percentage of the day spent
working since you woke up, and at the same time you plot it against
all the previous days so that you can see how you're doing compared
to the past. This gives you a percentile score at any point throughout
the day, which you can always meaningfully increase by working
more. Instead of only seeing how much work I'd done at the end of
the day, when it was too late to motivate me, I could see at any
moment how much I'd done, how good that was, and how much
more I could do if I kept at it.

---

88. http://blog.sethroberts.net/2011/05/01/percentile-feedback-and-productivity/

iOS work time today: 12:31:32

iOS Work Efficiency by Hour of Day
% Hours Spent on iOS Dev (compared to the past)

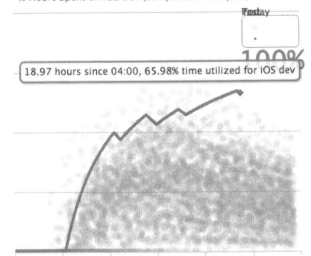

18.97 hours since 04:00, 65.98% time utilized for iOS dev

The first day of percentile feedback, I was so excited to see my work percentile climb that I did more iPhone app development in a day than I'd ever done before: twelve hours. This was exciting! And I measured that I got more done per hour, and had more fun doing it, the longer I worked each day. (I didn't have to beat my best each day, only my average.) I decided to set myself an ambitious challenge to excite myself even more: finish the app before May 1st, when Chloe and I would start preparing our move back to Silicon Valley to help start the Human Hacker House, when I didn't want to be spending all my time working any more. This would also get us launched before George's wedding on June 8th and before my twin brother's wedding on June 1st. I calculated that Scott and I would need to average thirteen hours a day between us to get it done in time. At the thought of coding all-out for four months, my eyes narrowed, my jaw jutted, and I smiled a maniac smile. *Let's see what I'm capable of.* (I remember this feeling well, because I felt it as soon as I thought of doing this book. Watch for it when you're picking goals—they should excite you!)

Through March and April, I was averaging 9.04 hours a day, every day. My focus was higher than ever, marred only by still-too-frequent email checking during code compilation pauses. During one week, I decided to see just how many hours I could do. 87.3[89], it turns out, not including three hours of hacking on Quantified Mind to help Yoni out. During that week, we fixed 122 bugs, built a ton of features, and sent out five new builds. Scott matched me with seventy hours of his own, and we blew all of our testers' minds with the new features we'd built. During another week where my target was seventy hours, I did a timelapse recording[90] of both my screen and my face, both as a demonstration to my friends that I actually would do that much real work, and as an aide to me to curb Impulsiveness—since I would look dumb if I pulled up beastskills.com to look at clapping handstand pushup training advice or Googled for the strongest dog. It was easier than I thought, though: I was already in line with my destiny. I overshot my quota of going out and being social five times a week, did an average of 125 pull-ups a day to even out my energy levels, and was sweet to Chloe 100% of days.

We did it: by May 1, we'd finished the app and submitted it to Apple for review. App Store Review usually takes a week, and if they reject the app, you change whatever they objected to, resubmit, and another week later you're live. We conservatively estimated four weeks for review time. But due to a thrilling app review adventure too frustrating to retell, we were still stuck in a review queue four weeks later when I started this book project and went off for ten days of wedding travel.

Everyone was frothing to know when we would launch, including dozens of bloggers to whom I'd sent prerelease copies and zillions of users and would-be users whom I had long ago teased into a frenzy with months of posting near-daily sneak peeks. Was I going to have to pull off the launch from the road while surrounded by

89. https://plus.google.com/110703832132860599877/posts/hwsETpJEtMk
90. https://vimeo.com/39643329

family, rehearsing my best man speeches, partying with bachelors, and keeping up with my book goals? Read on to the final chapter for the drawn-out conclusion!

Chapter Eight: Learning Anything

What to Learn

Motivation hackers can learn anything. They say that **anyone** can learn anything, but that's wishful thinking: anyone could, if he could bring himself to put in the time and effort, but if he doesn't know how to make himself do that, he can't learn his skill. But the motivation hacker knows how to not only do the learning, but to have fun doing it. Yes, fun. Learning should make you smile, not clench your teeth.

To hack motivation for learning, you apply the motivation equation as with anything else: use success spirals to increase Expectancy, learn something important to you in a fun way for high Value, avoid Impulsiveness with precommitment (especially the burnt ships technique), and focus on the learning process rather than the end goal so that you can learn ten new words by tomorrow instead of being fluent in Chinese in two years. But the other critical component is to use good learning methods, so that it's not only fun, but that you also make rapid progress.

I'll tell you of how I learned 3,000 Chinese words, knife throwing, skateboarding, lucid dreaming, public speaking, long-distance running, and CrossFit exercises during these three months, as well as a technique that I used in the past to help learn Spanish, Morse code, Braille, biases and fallacies, rational thinking techniques, social skills, anatomy, investing, cooking, what food labels actually mean, relevant phone and account numbers, some famous poems and chess games, how to deal with the police, sensual massage, and too many useless facts to mention.

As you build up your powers to learn anything, you'll need to be more careful in what you choose to learn—you'll have less of an "Ugh, this sucks" reaction to guide your studies, and so you'll need to keep asking yourself, "Is this worthwhile?" You need to be able to stop learning things when you realize they aren't useful or fun (population and GDP ranking of every country), while still never giving up on anything you do care about ("The Raven"), since that hurts your success spiral. A natural way to do this is to use short-term goals which you must always reach, but at which you can choose, in advance, to stop or re-up. A better way to do it is to use Beeminder's one-week delay in the ability to change your goal targets. And sometimes you can continue your goal of spending X minutes learning daily while switching out what it is you're learning in the event of horrifying boredom.

3-Month Projects

During the writing of this book, I wanted to learn things that were exciting, useful, and wouldn't take much total time. The largest of these was Chinese: I figured that in thirty minutes a day, using the new Skritter Chinese iPhone app that I was about to launch, I could learn to write 3,000 new words, or one every fifty-four seconds. This included learning and remembering 95% of these words at any given time, as well as reviewing all of the characters and words I already knew using its spaced repetition learning system. (More on spaced repetition later.) Now, I'd already been learning Chinese with Skritter for years, although not consistently, and I knew how to write 2,605 characters and 4,268 multi-character words. I could learn much faster than a beginner. It was time to broaden my vocabulary, I decided. So I put a goal of thirty-three words per day on Beeminder, made a routine whereby I got to Skritter in short chunks in fun places (the park, the hammock, the Papasan chair, in bed as I fell asleep), and stopped thinking about it. The difficult learning was ahead, but as far as my planning was concerned, I was already done. Next!

Skateboarding would be different. Not only did I not know how to skateboard, but I had no idea how to learn to skateboard, or whether it would be hard, or where I would get a skateboard. To begin, I did my usual precommitment trick of mentioning everywhere that I was going to learn to skateboard this summer. The usual lucky break happened: my new housemate Alex, who like a Santa Dumbledore is always happy to share his millions of fascinating artifacts, had a skateboard, a longboard, and an electric longboard[91]. He told me I could borrow them anytime and hustled me out to the driveway to show me how to use them. I could barely stand on the boards, and when I turned the electric longboard to its slowest setting, two miles per hour, I fell off again and again. *This is going to be hard*, I thought. *I might have to spend more than ten minutes a day.* (I did not think, *I might not be able to do this.* Practice learning things exposes this for the absurdity that it is, whether it's skateboarding or calculus.)

The next day, though, I woke up at six in the morning, carried the longboard down to the park while studying some Chinese, and then got ready for failboarding. To my surprise, I started cruising around right away. Exhilaration! Sage grin! I was inefficient, couldn't yet turn much, and almost ran over some dogs, but I knew this was going to be easy. I would have to work on my technique with Alex's help, but that would come, and eventually I'd be able to go ten miles. The hardest part would be to start saying "longboard" instead of "skateboard," which was hipness I knew not. That morning, I boarded back home into the sunrise and knew success. Next!

The story of knife throwing is the same as skateboarding. I sucked and couldn't get it for the first week. I mentioned this bemusement to my friend Alton, and he brought over dozens of better practice knives and showed me the technique better than I was getting from YouTube videos. Within that day, I was hitting 70% of the time with the bayonets from thirteen feet, almost at my 80% goal already. Delightful! When that knife thuds into the target zombie head, there wells a giddy feeling of badassery. *Why have I not done this before?* Within four days, I'd already taught two house parties' worth of people how to do the throw, as if I was some expert, and they also began to rock. I knew that with five minutes of practice each morning as I got home from skateboarding, I'd be plenty

---

91. A longboard is like a skateboard, but longer. An electric longboard has a motor, so you can go twenty miles per hour without pushing with your legs.

awesome in three months, and I set an informal goal of hitting at 80% from 28 feet instead. Next!

Lucid dreaming (where you realize you're dreaming and can control your dreams) was another skill which I had always wanted to learn and which doesn't take much time. I had known about it ever since I read about it on Wikipedia in senior year of high school and that night went on to have my first lucid dream, where I realized that if I was being whipped as a galley slave in a pirate ship, which doesn't actually happen in real life, then I must be dreaming and could do anything I wanted. I smashed out of my chains, Supermanned up through the deck of the ship, kicked the mast in half for good measure, and then flew across the ocean to discover a mountain island filled with giants and the ruins of their gargantuan temples.

Delighted, I thought I might have such adventures every night, but it wasn't that easy. I only became lucid once every couple months, I had limited control and often lapsed out of lucidity, I'd get too excited and wake up at the good parts, and my dream recall sucked. I forgot about deeper dream exploration and just switched between flying and sex in almost all of my lucid dreams.

Even from my brief reading that first day, I knew that lucid dreaming is a skill that just takes practice, the same as any other skill—and since most of the practice is done while you're asleep, it doesn't even take extra time. The Value is high, since the dreams are so much fun—a great lucid dream can provide days of excitement. Delay is not too long, since you can often start having lucid dreams the night after you read about them. Depending on routine, Impulsiveness might be high after waking when you should fill out your dream journal, or throughout the day when you should do reality checks, or as you're falling asleep when you should mentally condition yourself to have a lucid dream, but for me those were not impulsive times. I think I didn't have motivation to practice just because Expectancy was too low. Lucid dreaming was harder than I had first guessed, and so I had been discouraged.

When starting this project, I knew what to do about my low Expectancy: read a book on lucid dreaming by someone who is great at it and writes as if it's easy, then follow the author's advice to practice it. How-to books make things seem easier than they are, which can kill motivation once you follow the advice half-heartedly and then don't see any results. But they're great for getting you started, and if you actually do the things you're supposed to, then you get the great results you were promised (even though it's harder than the author made it out to be—after all, if he's writing a book on it, then he probably had an easier time learning it than most people will[92]). So I read *Lucid Dreaming: Gateway to the Inner Self* by Robert Waggoner, skipped the precognition and shared dream chapters, and had three lucid dreams in the first four nights involving wrestling centaurs, teleportation, morphing dream characters into other people, and asking dream figures for advice.

I started narrating my dreams using my phone's dictation feature every morning after I woke up, and my dream recall increased from less than one a night to 1.9 a night, with vivid detail instead of confusing plot holes. I started doing a reality check of smiling and shooting awesome rays from my eyes at things throughout each day. I started mentally affirming that I was about to have a lucid dream as I went to sleep, and visualizing previous dreams but with lucidity cues whenever I woke up during the night. I set dream missions for myself, so that instead of flying, I could ask inventor Elon Musk[93] for great insights on the future of science and direct extra muscle construction nutrients toward my pecs.

This is a good strategy for learning many things:

1. Get excited about a skill.

2. While you're excited, make time and hack up motivation to practice it.

3. Learn how to practice it from reading or from a teacher.

4. Start doing it right away.

---

92. A reader pointed out that you should have the same skepticism towards this book and me. Well, this is ironic.

93. Elon Musk: the super successful entrepreneur and engineer upon whom the character of Tony Stark from Iron Man was based. After selling PayPal, he is simultaneously disrupting the electric car industry and the private space industry, as well as working on solar power and talking about replacing high-speed trains. I would wonder who he talks to in his dreams for inspiration, but I don't think he ever sleeps.

It's simple if you don't skip any of these obvious steps. If you do skip steps, like setting aside time, designing a motivating environment, or starting now as opposed to the dread later, then it's hard. If your schedule is already full, then you might need to save the goal for later. You'll then need a trigger: something with enough spark to start a goal that you've grown accustomed to putting off.

My trigger for improving my public speaking came when I realized that I would have to give two best man speeches and a meetup talk in June, each to more than a hundred people. My previous public speaking style, with much smaller audiences, was, "It's not important, so just wing it." I had no problem starting now, reading several articles, and making time to practice when I needed to be good at it right away.

You can often manufacture this type of trigger: sign up to do something you don't know how to do in the hyperbolically discounted, not-so-scary future. When the time comes, you'll have to learn it. You're sending your future self a motivation bomb.

I did this with my marathon training. I had always wanted to be able to run without stopping, but I had never put in the time. I had thought of myself as fit and fast, but after I had to run five miles down a mountain to make a Skritter meeting for which I had mixed up my time zones, I realized not only that this was the furthest that I'd ever run, but also that I was not fit, fast, or able to move afterward.

When I started this book two weeks later, I said, "At the end of these three months, I will run a marathon." My Human Hacker Housemate Janet, a former Ironman triathlete and national-level competitive speed skater, agreed to coach me. I registered for the race (and a 5K, too—why not?), wrote it into my book, and told everyone I would do it. This was all easy, since I figured that the hard training would be weeks away, and I'd deal with it when I got to it. Nope. Janet had other plans.

"Here is your thirteen-week training plan. You want to train for a marathon from scratch in three months, which is too short. You also want to drop your 5K time by five minutes and increase your bench press by sixty pounds. And you only want to train for eight hours a week. And you don't want to get injured. And you don't want to be too tired to work. This is unrealistic. So you will have to train in intense bursts of many different exercises to do it. You need to go to the 6:30am CrossFit classes at Planet Granite, buy better running shoes and a jump rope, learn twenty-five new exercises, and unlearn nine exercises that you learned wrong, including your running—you look like a penguin with that much left-right pivoting. You need to sleep more, eat better, and do thirteen Pain-Free stretches[94] each day. I will teach you. You start today: longboard two miles to Sports Basement, buy running shoes, and run back."

So much for easing into it. At least I committed before I knew what I was getting into.

It is not easy for me to learn new movements. Of the few lifts I had been doing the previous fall—squat, deadlift, press, and pull-up—only my pull-up had good form. The rest I'd thought I was good at, but it turns out my form was bad enough that I was using the wrong muscle groups. Learning from books and videos was not working, so the coaching was essential. Even with knife throwing and skateboarding, I was literally starting off on the wrong foot until someone corrected me in person. And of all the training plans I had devised in the past, only one worked well past the initial gains: the crazy hundreds-of-pull-ups-a-day routine[95] suggested by Yoni, another Human Hacker Housemate. I say that I'm confident I can learn anything, but that process includes finding people to teach me for things that I don't pick up easily. I didn't need a public speaking coach or a lucid dreaming coach, and I can learn cooking from books, but I bet my handstands would be a lot better right now if I hadn't been training solo this whole time.

Another thing I had to learn was how to write a book. The longest thing I had ever written was a sixteen-page college paper for

---

94. The stretches are not pain-free, it turns out; you are just supposed to feel pain-free after you do them—that is, if you're not sore from learning a new lift every third day and sprinting until death three days a week. To learn more about the stretches, ask Janet: http://janetchang.com/

95. I had been stuck at fifteen pull-ups max for years, despite all kinds of training. I did 200 pull-ups a day, in easy sets of then throughout the day, for eight days, then rested four days and tested again at twenty. I got up to twenty-seven after another four months of 125 a day.

my honors thesis, and that took weeks and didn't have to be readable by anyone. How would I write an interesting book with 50-100 pages in three months while enjoying the process?

The day before I started writing, I spent three hours reading a few writers' blog posts and hitting all of the highest-rated topic threads at writers.stackexchange.com. Then I bought four books on writing that would kick off my read-twenty-books goal and committed to spending no more time reading writing blogs until I was done with the first draft. The process seemed simple enough: make a great writing environment, plan what you'll write first, write a target number of words of it every day, and don't show anyone or edit until you're done with the terrible first draft. Then, when editing, there were many specific tactics for rewriting it to be good, most of which distill to using a few, good words instead of many mediocre ones. *Sure, I can write a thousand crappy words in a couple hours each day. Then I'll cut out 30% of them and it'll be brilliant.* I determined that there wasn't much conscious practice that I needed to do, since the advice was all to stifle the conscious impulse to edit while writing. All the hard practice would come later.

Many writers, first-timers or not, talk about crushing self-doubt when writing. That must suck—writing is hard enough. I enjoyed it with limitless confidence, even without hardly any of the practice that everyone recommends. I'm not saying that I wrote a great book and that I'm a good writer, just that I knew that I would finish and then I would edit and re-edit and that nothing would stop me. I couldn't guarantee quality or readership, just excitement throughout the process.

A lot of people want to be writers, but don't want to write: they are seeking prestige on a borrowed goal. I wondered if this was true for me. I did remember that I enjoyed writing bad poetry back in high school Writer's Workshop, and I noticed some very high happiness pings while I spent a day writing all of the launch announcements for Skritter, which made me think that it would be a good goal. When I continued to measure high happiness levels every time I caught myself writing this book, I knew it was real. Writing rocks.

Anki

If you want to learn facts, then you should use a spaced-repetition system (SRS). You break knowledge you want to acquire into short answers to tiny questions, and then you make digital flashcards of those in an SRS program, which will then prompt you to review them at the most efficient time for strengthening your memories: right before you were in danger of forgetting them. You learn fast, you remember almost everything, and it's easy to turn into a daily habit that can deliver massive piles of knowledge in a few minutes a day.

Say you're learning Spanish. Now, not everything of learning Spanish should be learned as a fact with an SRS. Your pronunciation will best improve from actual conversation, and you'll want to read and write longer pieces to get context for the words you're learning. But part of learning any language is learning a lot of vocabulary, and SRS makes vocabulary learning easy. You put in the time each day, and you get a big vocabulary.

I bring up SRS not only because it's a great way to learn facts, and because learning facts is a large part of many goals, but also because it's easy to hack motivation with an SRS. SRS programs give you daily stats on how much progress you're making, how much time you're spending, how many reviews you need to do to stay on track, and how well you're remembering what you've learned. It's trivial to set measured goals for yourself, whether it's in Beeminder or not, whether you're aiming to learn X items per day or spend Y minutes studying. There's no Delay, since you get to learn useful information every day. With many SRS programs now being mobile apps, it's often easy to make time to do some reviews wherever you are, when Impulsiveness is lowest (commuting, waiting for people, after breakfast). Expectancy will be high: as long as you start slow, you'll automatically get great progress and start a success spiral of steady progress, since there aren't many reviews to do at first. And if you pick what you want to learn well, then the Value of what you're learning will be clear, and doing the reviews can even be fun.

If you're wondering what SRS program to use, you should choose Anki, which is a free desktop app, web service, and Android app, with a $24.99 iPhone app. Its flashcard system is versatile enough that you can learn just about any facts with it. I've used it to learn many things, including Spanish, cooking, and sensual massage. (To learn skills like sensual massage, it helps to think of the question as the cue of what just happened and the answer as what to do next: "Q: Second half of chest circulation, after pressing up to the neck?" "A: Lightly press back down the sides to the abdomen.") I've also used Anki to start learning many things which turned out to be useless, which I then deleted, like extensive geographical details on every country in the world. That's the first mistake to avoid with SRS learning: don't learn things which are not Valuable to you.

If you are learning Chinese or Japanese, then you should use my startup's app Skritter instead, since it's better than Anki. You don't have to make your own flashcards; you just tell it what textbooks or words you want to learn, and it makes them for you, with richer prompts than you could do with Anki. This highlights the second mistake of SRS learning: don't spend more time encoding and studying a fact than it will save you. If it takes a minute to make a flashcard and two minutes to learn it for life, then you should only learn things that will eventually save you more than three minutes of looking them up. If, as is average on Skritter, it takes just fifty-four seconds to learn an item, then you can profitably learn anything that will save you more than fifty-four seconds, which is any Chinese or Japanese word that you expect to encounter a few times (depending on your speed with a dictionary).

There are eighteen more classic SRS mistakes which you should avoid; read about them, and how to formulate SRS prompts, on the SuperMemo site[96]. But the biggest mistake is not listed there. It has killed more SRS study habits than all the others combined, and it will kill yours, too, if you don't hack it. It happens when you get behind on your studies and get buried under a mountain of all your overdue reviews.

---

96. http://www.supermemo.com/articles/20rules.htm

Because an SRS program models the actual strength of memories in your mind, which decay over time, it doesn't get to control when those memory items become due for review: they're due when you're about 10% likely to forget them. If you go on vacation, or forget about your reviews, or pause your studies when some big project looms, then those due reviews keep building up. Instead of spending fifteen minutes to review 200 old items and learn twenty new ones (the fun part), you spend fifteen minutes to review 240 old items from a week ago, and then another fifteen minutes for the next 240 old ones from six days ago, and another fifteen minutes, and another fifteen. You've studied for an hour, you're still not caught up, and you didn't get to learn anything new— and you forgot more of those overdue items than usual, too. You eventually push through it and get back on track, but it wasn't any fun. The next time it happens, you've learned to dread the overdue review mountain. Sooner or later, you'll give up rather than climb it, your SRS habit will die, and you'll lose all the knowledge you had so efficiently memorized.

This is unfortunate, because it's all in your head. Each review you do strengthens your total knowledge—learning isn't just adding new items. The number of reviews due is a guideline for you, not something you're graded on. And doing overdue reviews is often slightly more efficient than doing them on time—just a little more frustrating[97]. Yet if you are human, you will naturally get behind and then stress out about being behind.

The motivation hacker will not let this happen. Instead, she will focus her Expectancy on the process: "spend an average of fifteen minutes per day on Anki." She'll structure her goal to be strict enough to keep herself on track and flexible enough to achieve while still having a life. (Beemind it.) She'll build up her success spiral slowly so she doesn't fall off, make sure she's setting aside time to study, and keep an eye on what she's learning to make sure that it actually matters to her instead of realizing too late that she's added too many useless facts. And when she does spend six days meditating in a monastery with no chance to study, she'll over-

---

97. http://www.supermemo.com/help/fi.htm#FAQ

review beforehand and consistently review afterward, not paying much attention to the due reviews. And before you know it, without hardly trying, she'll know Russian, American Sign Language, human neuroanatomy, a thousand jokes, all useful account and telephone numbers, a poem for every occasion, a big-picture history of the world, and enough machine learning techniques to teach a robot kung fu.

Chapter Nine: Task Samurai

Dwarf Dishes

"Aren't you going to shower?"

"I just showered."

"What? Really? But you just... that was fast!"

This conversation is as reliable as a "fine" after a "how are you?" with every test subject who has witnessed one of my speed showers. I often shower lazily, lost in thought for fifteen minutes. But sometimes I've got something to do, and I want to shower quickly so I can go do it. Telling myself to shower quickly leads only to daydreaming. Making it a challenge to see how fast I can shower, however, leads to glory. My best shower time used to be 1:54 from entering to exiting the bathroom, clothed. While writing this chapter, I was tired and dirty from hours of working out this morning, but I showered in 1:37—new record!

If you have a Valueless task you need to do, then make a game out of it so that it challenges you. Get into flow. In *The Hobbit*, Bilbo's dinner dwarves did hundreds of dishes in no time by turning dishwashing drudgery into a dish-tossing song. Face boring tasks by imagining yourself as a badass Viking samurai who is called to fight chores. Fill in tax forms with serif handwriting. Timebox laundry. Use your non-dominant hand to take out the garbage, with your other hand behind your back. Floss blindfolded. Send a pesky email on only one breath of air. Clean a room while wearing a gi and listening to Dethklok. Challenge yourself to finish every overdue task today so you can go out and set something on fire tonight. Do some dwarf dishes.

Strategies

You probably already have a task management system that works well for you so that you know what to do next, you don't have to worry about what you're going to do later, you get everything done on time, and you're not stressed out about it. Good; that's what you want so you can spend your energies on things that matter. If you don't have a system, or if your system does not work as described, then you need a new system. There are no shortage of long books and short blog posts with equivalently good suggestions, so take your pick. Here are a few, if you need them:

• Getting Things Done: http://zenhabits.net/the-getting-things-done-gtd-faq/
• Zen To Done: http://zenhabits.net/zen-to-done-ztd-the-ultimate-simple-productivity-system/
• Final Version: http://www.markforster.net/
• Autopilot Schedule: http://calnewport.com/blog/2008/04/07/
• Four Quadrant To-Do list: http://sidsavara.com/personal-development/nerdy-productivity-coveys-time-management-matrix-illustrated-with-xkcd-comics

If you have a good system and it's still not working because you don't follow it, then build a success spiral around it. Take almost every task out of it, and then *always* do the remaining tasks. As you get more consistent, slowly add more tasks to that system (if they're worth doing). Tend your success spiral carefully, and eventually you will be able to do arbitrarily many tasks without furrowing your brow in despair or even annoyance. Once tasks afford only accomplishing and never putting off, you don't have to spend any of your motivation on running your life.

The Fool's Defense

Another good strategy for defeating Valueless tasks is to not do them. Sometimes this is easy, but not always. One strategy discussed earlier is trading icky tasks to people in exchange for tasks where you have a comparative advantage. Another strategy is to batch these tasks and do them less often, like sending mail, buying and preparing food, or having meetings. A third is to pay other people to do them: friends, personal assistants, virtual assistants, etc. You can often trade money for time, and the trade makes more sense when the time would be grudgingly spent.

A fourth strategy is the Fool's Defense: you signal your inability to perform a task in the hopes that someone else will then take care of it for you. An example defender is the professor Randy Pausch, who refused to learn to use the copy machine so his secretary would never expect him to make his own copies. This is okay, since his secretary gets paid to do things he can't do.

Another example which is perhaps not so moral is that of the mathematician who pretended to be unable to perform basic tasks such as doing laundry, cooking food, remembering appointments, or even finding his own apartment so that his wife would exasperatedly do all of these things for him and he could have more time to spend on math. In reality he was unfairly imposing on his wife, since he did know how to do these things, but that's what he had to sacrifice for his art.

I won't go into the ethics of mooching or the game theory of signaling inability as a substitute for negotiating the trading of tasks—those are things you'll have to decide for yourself—but note that you probably already do this already, whether you have your girlfriend crush spiders for you or whether your roommate has to fix the WiFi when the router acts up. If you're comfortable feigning helplessness ironing shirts, then you might consider developing a reputation of never answering emails. You'd save time and focus for more important things, and people would learn to deal with your eccentricity.

Chapter Ten: Experiments

Measure Your Results

Entrepreneurs, management gurus, and scientists all like to quote other entrepreneurs, management gurus, and scientists saying things like "You make what you measure[98]," "What gets measured, gets managed[99]," and "If you cannot measure it, you cannot improve it[100]." There's now a community called Quantified Self[101] which extends that idea to personal measurement for personal improvement. If you want to save money, you should track your spending. If you want to get stronger, it helps to track your workout performance. And if you want to improve your motivation, your focus, your happiness, or your productivity, then you should measure those things, because otherwise you won't know what's working.

You say, "I know what works for me!" Perhaps you do. Most of us don't, though. Kahneman's evidence[102] shows that we suck at remembering and predicting our own well-being. We as a culture still ignore this empirical evidence, recommending to live our lives so as to avoid deathbed regrets.[103] Deathbed regrets are like Hollywood films: they stir passions for a couple hours, but are poorly connected to reality. They are not good criteria for a well-lived life.

And it's not just in the realm of happiness where we are blind and claim to see. Whether it's success in business, fitness, diet, relationships, health, or productivity, there's a fad for that. The degree to which the next fad leaves us more successful than the last fad, combined with how contradictory the two are, shows how much

---

98. Some early HP executive: http://paulgraham.com/13sentences.html#f3n
99. Probably Peter Drucker, management consultant.
100. Lord Kelvin, physicist.
101. http://quantifiedself.com/
102. If you still haven't seen it, I'll link it again: don't miss this TED talk: http://www.ted.com/talks/daniel_kahneman_the_riddle_of_experience_vs_memory.html
103. http://sidsavara.com/personal-development/life-regrets

truth fads contain: not much. Most of a fad's contents are a sticky mixture of stories that sound good enough for us to believe them. There's a little bit of truth in each fad, but without struggling to carve out that truth from its sticky story goo, we'll be stuck switching fads altogether instead of preserving what worked from the last attempt. And the parts that work are different for different people—you can't trust anyone else to seek this truth for you.

If you want to improve, you can do it in two ways. The first is what everyone does: try something, and then decide whether it was worthwhile based on remembering-self hunches (or skipping the evaluation altogether and calling sour grapes if you failed, sweet grapes if you succeeded). Why, of course it was worthwhile to learn the guitar / compete in a triathlon / have kids / travel the world! And that unfinished movie script, well, it must not have been fulfilling or you would have finished it, right?

We tend to pick a destination, arrive somewhere else, and then be thankful we ended up precisely where we did, unaware of all the other places we could have gone, and more importantly, the other paths we could have traveled. This automatic contentment instinct comes in handy, since it keeps us at a baseline level of well-being[104] most of the time. But if we want to surpass the baseline well-being to which all our instincts strive to return us, we must seek the truth of what fulfills us more than average. If you're extraordinarily talented at introspection, you might be able to just meditate your way to an understanding of this. But the rest of us must use science. Enter the self-experimenter.

The self-experimenter improves by determining what works with simple experiments. For example, I wanted to improve my skin, but I didn't know what interventions would actually help. I started using facial cleanser on just one half of my face, body wash on just one half of my body, tracking when I showered and changed my sheets, and alternating weeks of wearing a clean T-shirt to bed. I then asked Chloe to help me count my zits each day, without telling

---

104. Unless your instinct is broken. Some people are tuned more towards the automatic dissatisfaction end of the dial and are unhappy wherever they go. They regress toward baseline well-being regardless of life circumstances, just like the rest of us, only their baseline is not high.

her which half was which. I analyzed the data and saw that body wash (p = 0.04) and facial cleanser (p = 0.02) both helped a tiny amount, washing the sheets did nothing, wearing a T-shirt did nothing, missing a day of showering did nothing, and missing multiple days of showering might have hurt a little bit. These results overrule many of my intuitions, and now I can save time not messing around with interventions that don't work and move on to testing some that might.

Whatever goals you pick, you should have some way of measuring the results. Many goals are intended to make you happier, so measure your happiness and see what is effective. If you're trying to get stronger, then measure how much stronger you're getting with each protocol you try so you can determine what's working. Trying to lose weight? Decide *in advance* how long you're going to try eating according to a nutritional philosophy, what the cutoff would be for much weight and body fat you would need to lose for it to be successful, do it for that long, then quit if it's not working or continue if it is. Be a scientist about it; a little rigor goes far.

The curiosity involved in running an experiment can help motivation, too. Now your reward is not just lowering stress for a month, but also discovering how to lower it again in the future. If you're as geeky as me, there can be as much Value in finding this truth as in the short-term result itself.

If you're like me and don't mind measuring lots of things, you can start to re-use measurements across different areas of your life to answer more questions. I can see that I feel healthier when I shower more, that I sleep better when I eat less, and that listening to music has no effect on my cognitive performance despite the huge effect on my mood. Almost half of scientific discoveries happen by chance.[105] If you measure only the most obvious possible result of pursuing your goals, you miss out on many of the truths that could surprise you.

105. Dunbar, K., & Fugelsang, J. (2005). Causal thinking in science: How scientists and students interpret the unexpected. In M. E. Gorman, R. D. Tweney, D. Gooding & A. Kincannon (Eds.), Scientific and Technical Thinking (pp. 57-79). Mahwah, NJ: Lawrence Erlbaum Associates.

Chapter Eleven: Mistakes

The Planning Fallacy

When hacking motivation, failure is expensive in terms of time coins, since you have to rebuild a lot of damaged Expectancy. But if you haven't had practice hacking motivation, then how do you avoid failure while attempting things you've never done before? Avoid these common mistakes as if your dreams depend on it!

The most common mistake is to fall prey to the planning fallacy[106] when setting up your success spirals. When humans estimate things like how long a task will take, their average-case and best-case predictions are almost identical, and their worst-case prediction is still more optimistic than what actually happens.

When you set up your success spiral, the planning fallacy will mess you up, because you'll think, "How often will I exercise? Oh, five times a week sounds doable. I'll start there." Then life happens. You catch a cold. A work project demands extra time. A birthday anniversary holiday vacation date thing comes up. The gym closes early on Sundays. You drink too much one night. Before you know it, you're toast, and your success spiral cracks.

You can't predict in advance what specific obstacles are going to batter you away from the gym, so you don't plan for any of them. But you should plan that *something* will make it harder than you can expect. A good hack is to take the outside view: ask yourself, "How long did it take last time?" or "How often did I work out last time?"

Plan for the worst and hope for the best. Start your success spirals small enough so that you're guaranteed to win, even if everything goes wrong. When I was starting success spirals, I thought I could average twenty minutes of Anki practice a day. I thought of the planning fallacy and cut that in half for a conservative estimate, and then performed a Hofstadter adjustment[107] and set my

---

106. http://lesswrong.com/lw/jg/planning_fallacy/
107. Hofstadter's Law: "It always takes longer than you expect, even when you take

success spiral goal for five minutes a day. I hoped I would do more than five minutes, and I usually did, but when life became a jungle with no room for civilized pursuits, I could hang on and do five minutes no matter how much I just wanted to sleep. Success spiral saved.

You can even set goals like, "Do at least ten seconds of journaling six out of seven days I'm near my computer." You'll hope to write 750 words[108] a day, but you'll plan for chaos, and when it happens, you won't get discouraged and quit writing. You'll still build a great habit.

Underhacked Motivation

Another way that overconfidence manifests itself is in how much motivation you decide to muster for a particular goal. In particular, you'll tend to not use enough motivation hacks. You'll think, "I already run sometimes without even pushing myself. If I set a schedule to run three times a week, and I tell a friend that I'm doing it, it'll be easy." Such optimism is human and must be fought. Set up more motivation hacks than you can ever imagine needing.

I can't count how many times I've told myself I could do something without needing to get too strict about it, only to rationalize quitting (or postponing) when the going gets tough. Neither can I count all the times that I've heard other people object to committing to a goal, reasoning that they shouldn't have to *force* themselves to do something that they *want* to do. They then come up with a single, clever trick from a book they just read, a silver bullet that they'll fire into the head of Akrasia Zombie[109] the next time he shambles up.

I don't know about you, but if I'm going to face a zombie, especially one that ate me last time I played, I'm going to want more than one bullet, and I'm going to want to fire them from range

---

into account Hofstadter's Law."
108. http://750words.com/
109. akrasia: the state of acting against one's better judgment. See http://wiki.lesswrong.com/wiki/Akrasia

instead of waiting until he's within brain-smelling distance. I'm going to hack motivation way more than I expect I'll need to, and I'm going to do it up front when I'm feeling most excited about my goal. I'll precommit, I'll burn ships, I'll create a motivation-only environment, I'll start self-tracking to keep myself honest, I'll find ways to make it more fun, and I'll precommit some more. I might only need one bullet to achieve my goal, but if I fire off fifty rounds in every possible zombie hiding spot while the sun is still up, I'm not only more likely to survive and win the goal, but I'm also going to have a lot more fun along the way knowing that nothing can stop me.

It's not fun to force yourself to work towards your goals. Don't rely on willpower, don't fall prey to overconfidence, and don't think that overbuilding your motivation structure somehow means that you're incapable of doing what you want to and should be able to do naturally. Once you have the success spiral of Richard Feynman or Tim Ferriss or Michael Jordan, you can skip the Beeminder and Just Do It. Until then, realize that everyone you see shining with competence and productivity either built great habits over a long period of time or has a mess of dirty dishes and buried insecurities hidden behind the rippling abs.

Unambitious Goals

I've said it before in Chapter 6, but I'll say it again in case you missed it. Avoid running after the wrong goals. The motivation hacker learns to run fast, and if he goes the wrong way, he'll end up far from the life he wanted. And if he makes himself excel at something he doesn't like, he'll override the natural pain indicators and push until he hurts himself. Always accomplish what you set out to do, but stop after any milestone where you realized that you weren't enjoying the journey.

Don't make the mistake of picking goals that don't excite you. Practice on some easy stuff, sure, but then use these motivation hacking techniques to amaze yourself. Do something crazy. It's much easier to do something hard and exciting than to do something easy that you merely **probably should**. "Eat 100% paleo for a month" is easier than "eat vegetables twenty times and eat processed food only four times" because it's more exciting. Both of those goals are specific, immediate, and (mostly) approach-oriented, but the second may not be challenging enough.

This is easy to mess up if you don't explicitly follow Dr. Steel's CSI Approach (setting Challenging, Specific, Immediate, Approach-oriented goals). "Eat more paleo[110] for a month" is not specific enough. "Eat only vegetables this month" is too challenging, and "Eat vegetables once a week" is not challenging. "Eat 100% paleo" has time problems (starting and stopping when?). "Don't eat modern foods this month" is okay, but it's less helpful in telling you what *to* eat, and it feels less noble to avoid eating bad food than to eat only good food. Sometimes people are afraid to be specific about a goal because they're not sure what they want or what they'll be able to accomplish—what if they commit to the wrong goal? But without a plan, they're not likely to succeed; they should plan as well as they can and then set a time limit on the goal so that if it turns out to not be worthwhile, at least they can stop afterward. Stopping after you reach a goal is better than stopping before you start, during your pursuit, or never.

---

110. The paleolithic diet: don't eat any foods that our ancestors didn't eat 10,000 years ago.

Chapter Twelve: List of Motivation Techniques

Sources

The major motivation hacking techniques I use—success spirals, precommitment, burnt ships, and being a task samurai—are all recommended in many places, including Piers Steel's book, *The Procrastination Equation*, which details the motivation equation and dozens of clever research experiments used to develop it. Look there for more details and supporting science. Steel also suggests many other motivation-hacking techniques, most of which I have tried and found less useful for me personally. Some of them may work for you, though, so I'll briefly list them here in case you're looking for extra hacks.

I prefer to focus on achieving superhuman motivation instead of avoiding normal human procrastination. Every motivation hack I suggest anecdotally in this book is backed up empirically in Steel's— except for the ideas of summoning vast motivation surpluses to burn as fuel for max fun and of riding success spirals to the stars. The motivation hacker will realize that she needn't stop at getting in shape and quitting an email addiction. She will catch old dreams, discover new ones, and do anything she pleases.

Expectancy

Recall that Expectancy is your confidence of success. These techniques increase motivation by making you certain that you'll succeed.

• Success Spirals. Set yourself a series of achievable goals and then achieve all of them until you expect only success and failure is no longer familiar.

• Vicarious Victory. Surround yourself with motivated people (and avoid unmotivated people) to have their motivation rub off on you. If you can't change your friends, reading biographies of inspirational people is an easier example of this.
• Mental Contrasting. Visualize the success you want to achieve, then contrast it with the not-success you have now. (If you skip the contrasting step, it may be worse than nothing.[111] Add in implementation intentions[112] and process visualization[113] for more oomph.)
• Guarding Against Excessive Optimism. We all fall prey to the planning fallacy. This often destroys success spirals. When planning paths toward goals, you can expect the best, but plan for the worst so that you can still avoid failure even when everything goes wrong.

Value

Value is both how rewarding a task will be when you finish it and how fun it is while you're doing it. These are general ways to adjust what you're doing so that it's more meaningful and fun.
• Find Flow. Tasks which are too easy or too hard are not engaging, so find ways to make tasks challenging but possible. I think of this in terms of being a task samurai and doing dwarf dishes. Make a game of it. Compete against yourself, or against others.
• Find Meaning. Look for ways to connect tasks with major life goals, so that you can remind yourself why you're doing what you're doing. Set up extra reminders of these connections where you'll see them.
• Set CSI Approach Goals. SMART goals are out, and Challenging, Specific, Immediate, and Approach (not avoidance) goals are in. These goals should excite you (the Challenging and

111. http://psych.nyu.edu/oettingen/, although there is debate about the value of outcome visualization by itself.
112. http://www.sas.upenn.edu/~duckwort/images/publications/Duckworth Kirby_FantasytoAction_inpress.pdf
113. http://commonsenseatheism.com/wp-content/uploads/2011/02/Pham-Taylor-From-Thought-to-Action.pdf

Approach bits). The Specific and Immediate bits help with Impulsiveness, making sure you know what you need to do at any time. I find that input goals (study ten minutes daily) tend to work better than output goals (learn ten words daily).

• Optimize Energy. Everything is more fun if you're alert, not tired. Sleep well, eat well, get fit, guard your circadian rhythms, and avoid burnout. Cure energy lows with quality breaks, movement, sunshine, and good music. Match intensive tasks with periods of high energy.

• Productive Procrastination. If you can't bring yourself to do your main task, at least get some other things out of the way. It's not perfect, but perfect is the enemy of good.

• Create Rewards. When you succeed, celebrate it, either by congratulating yourself or giving yourself a treat. Treats can backfire if overused, though. I prefer victory dances, fist pumps, and grinning like an idiot.

• Focus on Passion. Know what you're passionate about, and steer your life towards those passions. Ask if your common tasks are connected to passion; ask if they're intrinsically motivating.

• Task Trading. This one isn't backed up by any research (that I know about), but it makes economic sense, and I love it. Trade tasks according to comparative motivational advantage so that each person is doing the tasks which motivates her more.

Impulsiveness

Impulsiveness is your susceptibility to delay for a given task: how likely you are to put it off and do something more pressing. Limiting Impulsiveness often means getting rid of the options to do other things.

• Precommitment. Choose now to limit your later options, preventing yourself from making the wrong choice in the face of temptation.

• Burnt Ships. A specific form of precommitment where you disable, remove, or destroy a distraction or temptation.

• Goal Reminders. Make external reminders of your goals visible, and actually look at them. Avoid failing at your goals just because you forgot about them.
• Timeboxing. Place limits on the time allowed to perform a given task, the shorter, the better. It's easier to ignore distractions when you know you can't finish your task if you give into them, and that you only have to focus on your task for a short time.
• Build Useful Habits. Make an autopilot schedule for yourself and put your goals into it, or add goals to existing routines.
• Schedule Play Before Work. Plan times to have as much fun as you can—this leads to more efficient recreation, and it also lets you focus on your goals during the other times, rather than just having low-grade leisure constantly tempting you as an option. Play hard.

Delay

Delay is how far off the reward seems to be. This is often hard to manipulate directly, but sometimes you can set yourself up to perceive Delay differently, thus scoring a big motivation win.
• Break Goals Down. Granularize big goals until the next achievement is right in front of you. Subgoals and sub-subgoals defeat Delay. This is what Beeminder does automatically: you get a target for each day.
• Plan Fallaciously. This isn't so much a technique as a phenomenon, and its effects on motivation aren't backed up by any research, either—just my experience with my startup and marathon training. The planning fallacy automatically gives you more courage to start by underestimating the time and effort required to achieve many unknown, hard goals. I think this is a good thing, as long as your goals are input-based and not output-based.

Chapter Thirteen: So What Happened?

Missions

Recall the list of missions I came up with for the summer. Here are the motivation hacks I used for each.

- Go skydiving: precommitment x 7.[114]
- Learn to lucid dream: precommitment, timeboxing, overconfidence.
- Learn to throw knives: precommitment, success spiral, timeboxing.
- Learn to skateboard: precommitment, success spiral, timeboxing.
- Write a book: precommitment, success spiral, burnt ships, Beeminder.
- Learn to write 3,000 new Chinese words: precommitment, success spiral, burnt ships, timeboxing, Beeminder.
- Read 20 books: precommitment, success spiral, timeboxing, Beeminder.
- Be best man at two weddings: precommitment.
- Go on 10 dates: precommitment, Beeminder.
- Hang out with 100 people: precommitment, success spiral, Beeminder.
- Help to build a successful cognitive testing website: precommitment.
- Help start the Human Hacker House: precommitment.
- Launch a hit iPhone app: precommitment, task samurai.
- Run a startup: precommitment, success spiral, timeboxing.
- Increase my bench press by 60 lbs: precommitment, burnt ships.

---

114. Precommitment is listed in all of these since I wrote them into my book and told everyone I talked to what I was doing, but for skydiving I precommitted in multiple ways.

- Train to run a four-hour marathon from scratch: precommitment, success spiral, overconfidence.
- Drop my 5K time by 5 minutes: precommitment, success spiral, overconfidence.
- Increase happiness from 6.3 to 7.3 out of 10: precommitment.

Here's what happened with each mission. I also include mission results extras, like videos and stats, on my website: http://www.nickwinter.net/the-motivation-hacker/missions

Skydiving

Jump out of a plane while screaming in terror.

When she jumped out of the plane right before me, Chloe made the loudest scream that her tandem skydiving instructor had ever heard. She kept her eyes closed during freefall; in the video, it looks as if she's sleeping. Despite this terror, she had a big smile once on the ground—a classic skydiving success story of facing one's fear of heights.

My over-pre-commitment strategy worked. I was cool and confident until I jumped. Everyone told me that the initial leap is the only scary part, and then it's fun and surprisingly peaceful. I see now that this is like what you might tell a child in order to pierce it with a gigantic bone marrow needle. I guess it was fun, but at the time I couldn't decide whether to pass out or throw up. I think it was the indecision that saved me long enough to get to the ground.

Skydiving instructors, pointing and laughing: "Now there's a face that says you had fun!"

Me, white as a bone with all its marrow extracted: "... nnnguhhh ..."

Chloe, running over to me: "Oh my God, Nick! You're so white!"

Me, if I were in a movie: "My tan hasn't landed yet."

Me, not actually James Bond: "... how ... you ... I ... jumped ... big ... loud ... throw up ... mmm ... hold me!"

I did the scary thing and gained more confidence, but I won't go outdoor skydiving again. Too much driving (it takes two hours to get there) and not enough action (less than a minute) make for low fun density.

Lucid Dreaming

Increase lucid dreaming and achieve three fantastic dream missions.

While wrangling with a slippery pull-up bar in a hobbit-sized, bright green doorway to the woodshop in my ancestral spawning grounds in Minnesota, I thought to myself, "Why am I trying to put this pull-up bar in the Rochester house? This is probably a dream. I should do something else!"

The dream started to go away, so I tried to focus on the nail hole in the bright green doorframe, and after a few seconds the dream congealed once more, allowing me to move on with my lucid mission. I decided to teleport to some place with a view.

I found myself at Dad's place in Salt Lake City, up on the mountains, looking across the valley. I was tempted to fly over the valley, but instead I took up an insane rifle of gratuitous power and sniped a bullet over to the mountains on the far side, fifty miles away—except I was the bullet, and I flew in seconds to the other side with the city and lake whizzing below me. Thinking about how awesome this was, I decided to bullet-fly further, and I flew around the world a few times in a second. (This was too fast for me to notice anything.)

Then I decided it would be awesome to burrow-fly through the earth, so I flew up and then shot down into the ground in the valley. I flew through the dirt for a while like some superhero mole, although I didn't get too much sensory impression during this. Then I shot up inside an absurdly fancy building where some rich people were having one of those parties you only see in movies, where everyone is ignoring a bunch of guys in tuxedos playing chamber music and there are two white marble staircases per capita. I burst through the floor, and everyone gaped. I didn't stick around but instead flew through the ceiling, overwhelmingly pleased with myself already for having such a great lucid dream and for puncturing the posh party. It was nighttime when I broke through the roof of this glorious Salt Lake City cathedral temple tabernacle thing, and there was a fatty moon in the sky. I thought, hey, I could teleport over there and explore the moon! But then I decided against it, because I feared that sudden teleportation might wake me up. What would be cooler would be to haul the moon to Earth! Then I would have dream continuity, and I would get the moon.

I started hauling the moon down to myself as if I were pulling it on an invisible moonrope, and it lurched closer and closer and loomed larger and larger. Eventually it was half a mile across and floating above the suicidal-skateboarder-slaying hill up to Dad's house. I hovered up above some parked cars, then charged up and flew at the moon. I smashed through and overshot by a mile. Mummified in moon dust, I looked back to see the damage. The moon had split into one big piece and a bunch of pulverized debris, and when I looked, it did that nuclear-explosion-vortexing-a-space-planet thing with the flat, radial pressure wave where I hit it. Moon destroyed! High-five, bro!

I started to worry that since this lucid dream was being so long and detailed, I would start to forget it if I kept going, so instead of trying to become a planet, I decided to go home and go to bed to end the dream. On the inexplicably short walk home, I reviewed what had happened in the dream so far so I'd remember. Then I was in my bedroom in the Human Hacker House, and Chloe was there sleeping. I suddenly wasn't sure if I was still dreaming, since this was so mundane, so I decided to do my reality check: smile at something and shoot awesome rays at it. In this case, I smiled and shot awesome rays at Chloe, who started glowing with brilliant power, and she stirred and woke up. Yes, still dreaming! Satisfied, I went to lucid sleep and woke up.

The rest of that morning was glorious. If only I could start every day so adventurously! My dream recall hit 1.9 per night, and after reading the lucid dreaming book and starting to practice, I averaged one lucid dream per week. In periods where I thought about lucid dreaming more, I had more lucid dreams. This is a case where the continual reminder to direct attention toward my goal made it happen.

In addition to the above dream, here is a list of lucid dream missions accomplished during the project (not counting non-lucid dreams, where I rampaged as a dinosaur, defeated the greatest swordsman in the land, and stopped a nuclear explosion):

- Flying (three times)
- Sex (three times)
- Teleporting (successfully once and unsuccessfully once)
- Giving Chloe radiant glowing power through awesome rays from my eyes (twice)
- Using awesome rays on a toilet
- Talking to Paul Graham (semi-successfully)
- Turning into a dragon (unsuccessful)
- Paralyzing a witch to save Hermione[115]
- Wrestling a centaur
- Morphing dream characters into other people
- And asking dream figures for subconscious answers to life questions.

My dreams never used to be this cool! I had set my success criteria as doing three missions, and I blew past that.

After the project, I'm going to keep practicing lucid dreaming. I talked to my friend Ben Reitz the Dream Master, and he added even more ideas for my list of things to do in lucid dreams, which now consists of:

- Becoming a bear[116]
- Engaging in supernatural combat
- Exploring other planets
- Becoming a planet
- Being a sorcerer
- Riding a dragon

---

115. Not the normal *Harry Potter* character, but the Hermione from *Harry Potter and the Methods of Rationality*: http://hpmor.com/
116. Since accomplished. Being a bear is just as awesome as it sounds.

- Talking to dead people (relatives, famous scientists, berserk dictators)
- Working through problems with Einstein
- Creating my own animals using primordial energy from my hands
- Sending healing energy to afflicted parts of my body
- Ritualistically shedding burdens
- Hypnotizing my waking self in self-improving ways
- Being an opposite gender
- Practicing Chinese
- Seeking transcendental enlightenment
- Discovering my totemic dream animal
- Doing the most amazing dance the universe has ever seen
- Witnessing the Big Bang
- Composing music
- Burping so loudly that I destroy the sun[117]
- Discovering mysteries at the bottom of the vasty deep
- Experiencing life in four or two dimensions
- Having a conversation with a copy of myself
- Seeing what I'll look like in twenty years
- Seeing colors I've never seen before
- Practicing parkour
- Being in two places at once
- Generating amazing startup ideas
- Pulling my dream self out of a mirror
- Diving into the sun
- Swimming with dolphins
- Mixing senses so as to taste colors
- Being inside a cartoon
- Transmogrifying into a cloud and raining down
- Running faster than sound
- Stepping through mirrors
- Stopping time

---

117. Since accomplished—actually, I unleashed a destructive burp during a total solar eclipse that then destroyed both the moon and the sun at the same time. Everyone stopped dancing after that.

- Flying with wings
- Traveling to another dimension
- Building a dream workshop that has doors through which I can enter continuous dream environments, like my science lab or my continuing adventure.

Knife Throwing

Hit a target from 13' 80% of the time.
- Average daily practice time: 5 minutes.
- People I taught how to throw: 30.
- Goal hit rate from 13 feet: 80%.
- Actual hit rate from 13 feet: 90%.
- Best streak from 13 feet: 41 in a row.
- Hit rate from 28 feet: 50%.
- Knives mysteriously vanished: 3.
- Knives thrown over the west fence: 40.
- Times I jumped over the west fence: 40.
- Arrows shot over the northwest fence: 1.
- Sandlot beast dogs over the northwest fence: 2.
- Times I jumped over the northwest fence: 0.[118]
- Cabbages accidentally destroyed: 6.

Throwing knives is so much fun, it's no wonder that it's the most popular American pastime, with the average person throwing for nearly five hours a day. If only! But it's almost as hard to understand why people do not throw knives as it is to understand why they watch so much TV. Everyone who tried it was able to do it, and all but one of them enjoyed it. It was easier than I expected to hit my accuracy goal after Alton taught me the basic technique. (Before that, I spent a week getting nowhere with YouTube videos and too-small knives.)

On the last day, when I went to test my final accuracy, I made a video[119] of myself throwing from the 28-foot distance. To make it

---

118. Those dogs don't sleep. *You* go get the arrow, Alex.
119. http://www.nickwinter.net/the-motivation-hacker/missions

more fun, I taped my phone onto the target to record the throws. It took me several takes, and I almost pierced the phone a couple times, but I got it. I then invented longboard knifethrowing, where you ride your longboard past three targets as you try to hit each one with a knife. It's like Yabusame, the traditional Japanese art of mounted archery, except for real people[120]. Awesome, right? This is going to blow up, let me tell you. Everyone will be doing it.

Longboarding

Be able to travel 10 miles on a longboard.

Because I had originally wanted to longboard as a way of getting around that wasn't walking or biking, I set my goal as longboarding for ten miles. To that end, I learned both goofy and regular footing from the start, so that I'd be able to switch between the two and have more endurance. Even after the first month, when I was able to go for short rides and not torpedo the board into the street every two minutes, I still couldn't go very far before the shin or calf from some 90-year-old man would teleport into my leg, displace my youthful tissue, twang in exhausted pain, and force me to limp home. Not good enough.

So I switched out my beloved Vibram toe shoes for icky running shoes, fixed my knee-bending and foot-pumping action with coaching from Skatemaster Alex, and kept practicing. I also taught two friends. Longboarding is harder than knife throwing, but I never fell. I think this means I wasn't training hard enough.

A week before the final test, I took the electric longboard on most of the route I would ride. If there is a mode of ground transportation more fun than this, I do not know it. I felt like the coolest human. It goes up to twenty miles per hour, which is sick fast for something with brakes like soggy gum. I also learned the answer to the eternal question of whether I can jump out of a moving vehicle and just run double-fast without falling over: not if it's going a whit faster than twenty miles per hour. Whew!

---

120. For real people as opposed to Tim Ferriss: http://vimeo.com/8611471

The ten mile mission was a success. I took it easy and averaged six miles per hour, including waiting on traffic lights, walking it past double-wide pedestrians, and climbing 300 feet. I'm not a great longboarder yet, but I can get around and have fun, and I can switch my feet while riding. This is sufficiently rad.

Writing a Book

Write a complete first draft of this book about motivation hacking.

My strategy of Beeminding a thousand-word-a-day writing goal, with $7290 on the line if I fell off track, worked too well. I finished the first draft of everything except this last chapter after five weeks of writing, realized my book was going to be a short one, paused my Beeminder, and sat around picking at the editing while wishing I had more writing to do. My daily routine unraveled a bit once it lost the morning writing session, and my average happiness was 0.5 points lower without it. I need to create more writing projects for myself. I love writing.

When I was a kid, my parents provided two examples: Artistic Writer Mom and Computer Engineer Dad.

Mom: "Look, I have painted a phoenix girl! Let us go to my photography showing and then the Repertory Theater play. Afterward, we shall play Boggle with Cathy and spawn dragons from Fimo clay. My 'egg horror poem' is going to be in a 9th grade literature textbook!"

Dad: "I am ahead on all my IBM ASIC[121] timing projects and have just pruned the apple trees. Wanna play apple baseball or construct rockets from tinfoil and match heads? After you finish your math homework, I'll write a Perl program to generate all possible solutions."

Both parents were happy, both paths were attractive, and both talents seemed, if not things I had, then things I could reach for. But it seemed as if you couldn't do both, as if you had to be either

---

121. ASIC: application-specific integrated circuit. These are complicated, custom chips in everything from Xboxes to satellites.

creative or logical; artistic or scientific; into books or into computers. (I don't know where I got this idea.) For a while, I wasn't into anything constructive. In senior year of high school, it was all about Writer's Workshop with Mr. Mahle[122]. In college, I was pulled to and fro by the latest fascinating classes, ending up with the computer scientists and letting creative writing go. I got serious about writing code and forgot about writing anything else while I did my startup. My choice was made.

That was silly. Why give up something I love? I may not be able to make a living doing two things at once, but from motivation hacking I've learned that I don't need to make a living from something to spend hours a day doing it. Never again will I tell parts of myself, "I don't have time for you." I now know how to make time.

And for the mission—how did the book turn out? Let me know! nick@skritter.com

Learning 3,000 Chinese Words

Go from 4,268 word writings learned in Skritter to 7,268.

Three months ago, I knew how to write 4,268 Chinese words comprised of 2,605 different characters. Now, forty-one hours of study later at twenty-seven minutes per day, I've learned 3,005 new words and 353 new characters, with a 91.7% retention rate. I've still got a lot to learn, but this is a big step for my written Chinese. For reference, the highest level of the old, too-hard Chinese proficiency test required 3,109 characters and 8,619 words. Counting literacy by vocabulary size is like dating based on physical attractiveness: you're eating the shallow crust of a deep pie, but it's tasty and everyone does it. It's not as if my next book is going to be in Chinese or anything—but maybe the one after that will be.

As predictable as this mission was, there were two surprises. The first is that learning so many characters in a row made me so

---

[122] Mr. Mahle would say that it's all about the red wheelbarrow glazed with rainwater beside the white chickens (referencing a poem by William Carlos Williams).

good at it that I freaked myself out. Normally in Chinese, you can't tell how to write a character you've never seen even if you know what it sounds like and what it means. You get some faint clues, but it would be like guessing the medical name for cheese poisoning is "tyrotoxism."

Here's an example: There's a character pronounced yǎng which means "to itch". How do you write it? Why, 痒 of course: the sickness radical 疒, plus it kind of sounds like 羊 (yáng: "sheep"). I guessed and wrote this character in three seconds and was on to the next prompt before I realized that I'd never seen it before. This was way better than my normal mode of infrequent learning, where each new character was a mystery.

The second surprising thing was how dependent I was on Beeminder to get me studying. I've tried to ramp up my Chinese self-study several times before. Each attempt whimpered off. Here is my Beeminder graph of word writings learned:

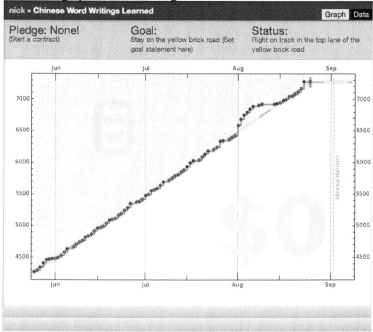

The points which hug the bottom of the line are days where I would have failed my goal if I didn't learn some more words by the end of the day. I commanded Beeminder to command me to study, and so I studied. It wasn't painful; I enjoyed the studying, but I just wouldn't study enough without help. There's one bump in the beginning of August where I motivated myself to get ahead, but it didn't last.

Reading Twenty Books

Read twenty fiction and non-fiction books on my reading list.

The Beeminder graph for reading twenty books looks similar to the 3,000 Chinese words graph, except there are about ten places where I jumped way above the line. That's what happens when I couldn't stop reading a great book. So about half the books fascinated me; sounds right. To see the graph and the list of books I read, check out http://www.nickwinter.net/the-motivation-hacker/missions. Was reading a book every 4.5 days as rewarding as I'd hoped? Yes, and more. The summer feels richer for the ideas and stories that filled it.

I gave up early on four books that I didn't like, and I never do that. Awareness of my purpose in reading helped me say no to boring books. I also had to trisect my favorite, *Cryptonomicon*, with two shorter books in order to stay alive on Beeminder. 1168 pages! I love it, but next time I set a book-reading goal, I'll make it time-based.

Reading books in parallel with my goals inspired me. Books on writing, motivation, willpower, and lucid dreaming hit the spot. Less obviously but perhaps more helpful were the tales of science fiction adventure, which reminded me to dare mighty things[123] for my next tech startup.

---

123. Teddy Roosevelt, "The Strenuous Life": http://www.bartleby.com/58/1.html

Public Speaking

Learn public speaking and pull off two great best man speeches.

The first best man speech was for my twin brother, Zach. Zach is a handsome, friendly guy who will fly across the country for a deal on a souped-up Miata you want to buy, drive it a hundred miles per hour back home, help you put another hundred horsepower into it, and then study for Monday's class. Out of a million friends I don't know why he chose me to be his best man, but I wasn't about to disappoint him. I hadn't been to a wedding since he and I were tapped, at age four, to carry a bridal train and spewed monstrous spittle when we realized that this was not a real train but some horrific prank name for part of a wedding dress.

I no longer had the excuse of being four years old, but I still had the wedding know-how of a four-year-old, but with less public speaking confidence. I challenged success to a duel by telling everyone that my speech was going to rock: "Bro! Bro? Bro. I got this." Then I snuck off to The Art of Manliness[124] to figure out what I was supposed to do and whether there were any more cruelly named things waiting to surprise me this time. Making a toast? *Which kind of toast?*

Turns out I should have read up on what it means to catch the garter.

The Art of Manliness gave me the essential tips I needed: thank the parents, tell a story about the groom which shows that he's a great guy but desperately needs a great lady to fill in for a particular character trait, make an appropriate joke, show how the bride completes him, and end with a quote and a toast. Not too hard, if you follow the first tip: prepare it in advance. Right! Well. Because I had to keep reading books, running, and learning Chinese while hanging out with every family member and preparing the Skritter iPhone app press campaign, then at the last minute needing to submit a bug fix update to the App Store, I found myself writing and memorizing the

---

124. http://artofmanliness.com/2008/07/22/how-to-write-deliver-good-best-man-speech/

speech[125] at two in the morning the day of the wedding while telling my brother that I was fixing some bugs.

The wedding was beautiful, everyone cried, and a little boy brought me the rings ribboned onto a small turbocharger[126]. I guess this is my brother's way of degirlifying things in revenge for the traumatic trainlessness of yore. Apart from the ceremony, I was rehearsing my speech all day, peeking at it on my phone when no one was looking.

Did you know that after the wedding ceremony, there's a whole separate part where you wait for a while, go somewhere else, and then resume the wedding but with even more people? Yeah, on top of the rehearsal, the rehearsal dinner, the bachelor and bachelorette parties, and the honeymoon. Complicated! I don't see any point to having a separate wedding reception except for making the best man simmer in a stew of his own nerves for a couple hours. Then you don't even give the speech, but instead everyone eats and looks at you sitting at a special table for an hour, and *then* you get everyone's attention and give the speech.

This is a pretty good design, but it could be scarier. If I were in charge, I'd make the best man have to give the speech at a random time so that terror can strike at any moment. He'd *have* to drink to survive the tension. This must be the point: to encourage more inappropriate, drunken rambling.

Anyway, after everyone ate for ninety hours, I got up and started orating. Funny part #1: laughter! Funny part #2: more laughter! Sentimental part #1: sighing! Funny part #3: they laughed at *that?* Sentimental part #2: everyone loves everyone! Optimistic part: murmur blanket. Forgot the quote and skipped to the toast and done. Hugged the glorious bro. Killed it. Received compliments the rest of the night and didn't see my phone again for hours as the text of my speech was passed around the acoustically underprivileged family flocks.

---

125. Read the speeches at http://www.nickwinter.net/the-motivation-hacker/missions
126. A turbocharger is an aftermarket car part that increases power to the engine and makes you cooler in exactly the way that bragging about your DTRLs (daytime running lights) will not.

Next I attended my Skritter cofounder and best friend George's wedding. George is a magnet with a million friends, too, but I stuck to him in college and didn't detach until Becca rescued him, so I got to be his best man despite the risk that I might tell the Crazy Sleepwalker Girl story[127] or the Crazy Arms Dealer Girl story.

I was still on the road for the week in between weddings, and still busy, but I managed to write and memorize this speech days in advance. George converted to Judaism for this one, and I worried about new sinister wedding traditions. All of those traps were for the groom, though; I had it easy.

My speech this time involved a funny story about a credit card, so I stole George's MasterCard before the wedding. I went out on the wedding dance floor in my fancy suit but with no shoes, which doubles one's confidence (try it!), and gave an even better speech than last time. After the toast ("May you never need to run again."), I presented George's own credit card to him and announced, "But you're definitely going to need this!" This dumbfounded him, and then we all laughed forever.

Later, after frenzied dancing and the younger brother cupcake duel and the part with the havoc chairs and the fire tunnel, I realized two things. One: weddings are not just pranks perpetrated against the guys who have to be in them. Two: I like public speaking.

That's crazy! This is Nick we're talking about! Remember how at eighteen he was too scared to order his own burritos in Taco Bell? That guy? If *he* now enjoys getting up in front of a hundred people, making jokes, and sharing tender emotions—if he can do that, then what can he not do?

I got a third chance to talk in front of 140 people this summer at a Quantified Self meetup in Berkeley. By now I knew that this was going to be fun. Talk about the cognitive testing self experiment that I did? Sure! An Ignite Plus talk where your thirty slides each advance automatically after fifteen seconds? Perfect! I went, I spoke, I conquered. This social confidence is real.

---

127. It involved a bed, panties, and a compromised and terrified George who turned out not to be schizophrenic.

Ten Dates with Chloe

Go on ten romantic dates with Chloe.

I'm still a beginner at the previous missions in this chapter, but I'm pro at boyfriending. The ten-dates-with-Chloe mission wasn't meant as a challenge, but as a failsafe to preserve a minimum level of attention to her in case I became too busy with the other missions. I spend much more time with her than that, so it wouldn't make a difference, right?

Turns out that if you demand to spend a romantic evening with a girl on a night where you're clearly too busy to do any such thing, and you call it a date, and you show the same affection you normally do, she opens triple the amount of romance receptors. She charges up with love until she glows! Then she dissipates it over the next several days with yearnful ring-finger waggling.

I could ask her whether we're closer now than ever before in our five years together, but I know what she would say[128]: "Gee, I don't know, Nick—why am I *not married* yet?" Then she would invent yet another emoticon for glaring at me and try to do the face that corresponds with that emoticon. Recent creations include ._. -_- ¬_¬ B| and the past-mock-anger-and-into-mock-bereavement :<

Anyway, we are. Closer together, that is—not married[129].

We ended up with thirteen dates: one a week. Score another one for Beeminder. You ask, isn't it unromantic to rely on a web application to tell you when you need to be romantic? I'll tell you what's unromantic: forgetting to do things like digging caves in strawberries to put blueberries in them and surprise your girl at her bus stop with a blind, no-biting taste test[130] to determine what double morsel you're holding in front of her mouth. Beeminder may be a robotic bee that you sic on yourself, but it will watch out for your girl's heart better than she will.[131]

---

128. Okay, I just asked her. "No!" "Why?" "Because we're *not married!*" B|
129. Not at the time of writing, that is. ;)
130. Strawberry: easy. Embedded blueberry: hard.
131. According to singer Billy Joel's 1983 hit "Tell Her About It", most girls will not tell you often when they wish you would be more romantic, because then it wouldn't be spontaneous.

Talking to a Hundred People

Have significant conversations with a hundred different people.

This goal didn't end up giving me extra motivation to socialize—I had meaningful conversations with 173 people, overshooting my goal of one hundred. I had been afraid of hermitting out, but between weddings, Quantified Self meetups, Human Hacker House events, the Ancestral Health Symposium[132], hiring interviews for Skritter, hiking trips, and friends visiting to throw knives, I have been more social than ever. It was fun to track the new people I talked to, though.

Quantified Mind

Hack on Quantified Mind and present to a hundred people about it.

This was not a well-specified goal. "Hack on Quantified Mind?" It's concrete, but it's not specific: how much time should I spend hacking? How many features do I need to build? And it's not immediate, either: there is no "when," other than "sometime during the three months." I wish I'd written this bad goal on purpose as an example of what not to do.

I did get some hacking in with Yoni when he had time to work on it, and we built a Data Minding feature where users can see powerful graphs of how their cognitive performance varies with different interventions. And I did give my Quantified Mind talk[133] to help promote it. But should I have hacked more? Did I meet my goal? Even now, it's hard to tell. Don't make vague, weasel-friendly goals. I did much better last year with this goal: "Work on Quantified Mind for three hours a week."

---

132. The Ancestral Health Symposium: a conference where sexy cavepeople get together and argue about just how much earlier you'll die for every gram of carbohydrates you eat.
133. http://quantifiedself.com/2012/07/nick-winter-a-lazy-mans-approach-to-cognitive-testing/

Human Hacker House

Do my part of writing content, organizing events, and helping housemates.

This goal also backfired. I didn't know in advance how many blog posts the six of us were going to write for the Human Hacker House, or how many events we would hold, or how much we would help each other with our projects, so I figured, "I'll do my part: as much as the others do. Then my goal will scale up to however much effort is appropriate. And I know keenly when I'm not contributing equally, so I won't just forget."

The other Human Hacker Housemates must have thought similar things, because no one wrote any blog posts! Janet set up the blog[134], Chloe designed it, Alex and I wrote the manifesto, we all brainstormed fascinating experiments to do and posts to write—and then we did a bunch of experiments and didn't write them up. Habit failure! I successfully did my share: one manifesto plus zero blog posts. I am shamed. Before I write any further, I will create the first blog post introducing this calories-and-weight-change experiment which Yoni designed. ... There[135].

The organizing of events went better. We held several, and I helped feed, host, and teach knife throwing. Did having this explicit goal motivate me to do this? I don't think so. Same thing with the helping of housemates on their own projects: I would have done that anyway. I did feel better about spending the time, though, having set it aside for these two purposes. Normally, without having planned to spend time helping out, I'd be looking at the time and wishing to get back to my real mission. I do recommend this sort of remember-to-be-human goal for anyone like me who might otherwise forget. I think most won't need it, though.

iPhone App

Manage launch publicity campaign and finish fixing all bugs.

---

134. http://humanhackerhouse.com/
135. http://humanhackerhouse.com/calories-weight-change-experiment/

Due to the funny App Store review jokes the review team pulled on us that I mentioned before, our iPhone app launch was a month late and aimed right in the middle of George's wedding. Hah, good one, Apple! Between moments of bachelor parties, best man duties, and the projects for this book, I was feral trying to maul last-minute bugs and coordinate my flock of bloggers. Human Hacker Housemate Eri, she who knows how to court press and raise funds, and Marjolein Hoekstra, Skritterer and social media maven, had given me some tips on pitching bloggers about covering app launches, and they'd worked almost too well: 25 of 27 Chinese language learning bloggers I talked to agreed to cover the app launch, along with many of the general tech and app bloggers. This was great for publicity, not so great for my sleep—this was the one time during the project when I wasn't getting enough rest.

Scott and I went back and forth about whether to prank George by releasing the app the morning of wedding and telling him during the best man speech. I thought it'd be hilarious, but Scott thought that we might need to be on hand in case something went wrong. Turned out we had to delay three more days anyway because Apple has a funny way of counting five business days. This was good, because Scott the Reasonable One isn't called that for nothing. "What could go wrong?" I had asked. "How much feedback could we possibly have to respond to in one day?" He said that since we didn't know, and since it was important, we should be prepared for anything. This was wise.

I woke up at three in the morning and pushed the Launch App button. It hit the App Store by four, and I updated the website, published the Skritter blog post[136], sent 15,000 emails to people interested in knowing when the app would launch, posted on Facebook, Twitter, and Google+, and thanked all of our testers. Emails started to arrive. This guy loves the app! That guy loves the app! This girl... sees a black screen right away where the intro should be? What?

One of the last-minute safeguards we put in to prevent a rare crash had backfired. For people upgrading the app to that latest

---

136. http://blog.skritter.com/2012/06/skritter-chinese-ios-app-launched.html

version, everything worked fine, so neither we nor our testers noticed[137]. But for people installing it from scratch, the intro didn't work. Nothing—black screen. It didn't crash, and there was a complicated workaround involving skipping the intro, signing up, and force quitting the app, but this was bad. This is the third thing you do in the app and there's no apparent way past it. If you did manage to skip it, we then asked you for $9.99 a month on the next screen. How classy! We might as well have put a button there asking for a one-star review. Disaster!

But what was this? Where were are all these five-star reviews coming from? Everyone who learns Chinese is some sort of detective / saint combo, apparently. Somehow tons of people were not only figuring out how to get past the bug and its sub-bugs, but also were hitting the App Store right away and saying how the app was perfect and sexy and that they wanted to kiss us but it would be weird. We managed an average rating of 4.4 out of 5 stars[138] for that version despite the bug. The Chinese language learning blog community went wild with Skritter reviews and the sound of Apple haters grudgingly shelling out for iPod touches just to run the app.

I wrote 154 emails, blog comments, Facebook responses, and tweets that day, along with going to the gym at 6:30am for my first CrossFit class and submitting a bug-fix update[139] to the App Store. This is the kind of exciting day that I craved. This is what I wanted. Yes.

Over the rest of the summer, we put together the Japanese version and are launching that a week after the end of this book project. This launch will be smoother.

---

137. App Review must have seen the bug and should have rejected this version, but perhaps they thought it would be another funny joke.
138. Overall we're up to 4.9 / 5 now that the demo bug is done.
139. Despite expedited review, this took another week to get through. Apple told us we now can't call the demo a demo or the free trial a trial. This last joke brought tears to my eyes.

Startup

Stay on top of Skritter work as cofounder and CTO.

Running a startup takes time. Fixing bugs takes motivation. This goal was not specific, but I had enough accountability to customers and cofounders that it was clear what needed to be done, and so I got it done.

You can find out more about Skritter at http://www.skritter.com.

Bench Press

Go from 1 rep max of 150 lbs to 210 lbs (I weigh 140 lbs).

Before starting this project, I had wanted to pick some strength training goal other than deadlifts. I was sick of deadlifts[140]! While participating in one of Alex's muscle sensor experiments, I was outbenched by a 71-year-old. I decided I needed to train to bench more so as not to dishonor my ancestors[141].

---

140. Janet made me do all sorts of deadlifts anyway. I ended up increasing my deadlift by twenty pounds, to 270.
141. My dad is ripped from doing living room exercises a few minutes a day for the last twenty years. My brother is constantly fit from sheer manliness. I have to do a

How much more? I didn't know, but I figured that since I hadn't done any pressing exercises in six months, I probably had lost some strength that would be easy to get back at first, and so if I increased my bench press by sixty pounds, this would be appropriately ambitious. With my goal set, I tested my max and found to mixed dismay that it was higher than it had ever been: 150 lbs, not the 135 lbs from last fall. Uh oh. This would mean I would have to hit 210 lbs, or 1.5 times my bodyweight.

I followed Janet's chaotic exercise regimen, ate many pounds of protein, got extra sleep, eradicated my left-right imbalances with the least pleasant workouts yet, and improved my technique. Janet had me doing sets with very low reps so as to allow for more training, often five sets of two reps with five minutes' rest in between. In total, I only did 112 non-warmup reps of bench press. After three months, I had gained 1.5 lbs of fat and 4 lbs of muscle. I approached the bench for my final test, bristling with muscle sensors[142].

I got to 190 lbs and couldn't lift anything heavier. I failed to increase my bench press by sixty pounds, instead only gaining forty pounds. Rats!

While I failed at my goal, I still grew stronger. Because my goal was an output goal (measured by results) rather than an input goal (measured by time or effort), I knew I wouldn't be able to control whether I succeeded, only whether I put in the time. I chose sixty pounds because it excited me, even though I knew that it might be too much. So I'm not too disappointed by my failure. I'll continue to train bench press after this, and I'll get to 210 soon.

Marathon

Build endurance from 5 miles to 26.2 while increasing speed by 10%.

I chose this goal because I wanted to be able to run fast for a long time, and running a marathon in four hours sounded like an

---

lot of work to fit in at the pool.
142. Human Hacker Housemate Alex Grey makes the wireless muscle sensors I used to measure muscle performance: http://somaxis.com/

exciting way to make sure I could do that. I had nearly killed myself on a forced five-mile run to get back home for a meeting the month before starting this project, and that was at a ten-minute mile pace. Before starting the project, I ran a pretest 5K to see more accurately where I was at. The good: I finished it. The bad: Everything hurt, and I limped home. The terrible: it took me 28:15, or 9:06 per mile, basically the same as the 9:09 pace I'd need for the marathon. I'd have to maintain my 5K pace 8.5 times as long.

Most people will train for a marathon using long, slow runs, averaging forty miles per week and training for five to six months[143]. A common guideline is to increase mileage by no more than 10% a week to get the body used to running longer and longer. I did not have time for this, and my starting endurance sucked, so Janet advised that I try doing high intensity interval training plus CrossFit metabolic conditioning workouts, with daily stretching, weekly runs of 5-10K, and a half marathon after two months. These exercises were very hard and unpleasant, but I did them all. In total, I only ran for sixty-nine miles, but running itself was only a small part of the training I did.

When it came time for the half marathon, which I ran in San Francisco with 24,000 other runners, I had no idea what to expect. The longest run I had done so far was 6.2 miles at a ten-minute-mile pace. Janet told me to run this in under two hours. Running a marathon in four hours is roughly equivalent to running a half marathon in 1:56:08[144], at least cardiovascularly, assuming one doesn't fall apart at the greater distance. I woke up at 5:30 A.M. and froze my way across the city to the second half marathon start. While waiting for the 8:30 A.M. go time, I chatted with the other runners, who all looked at me with pity when I told them about my training, as if I were an excited child about to step into the ring with Mike Tyson.

Then the race started, and I blasted past a thousand of them in my convertible shorts and dorky giant headphones. I hadn't noticed for the past two months because of the grueling interval training, but

143. http://en.wikipedia.org/wiki/Marathon#Training
144. http://www.coacheseducation.com/endur/jack-daniels-nov-00.htm

it turns out that running is fun! I started off conservatively slow, but as I kept feeling great, I sped up throughout the race. There were bystanders holding funny signs[145], bands playing, people giving high fives, and beautiful scenery to motivate the runners. I played a game where I would target someone ahead of me and make a micro-goal to pass him or her—take that, Delay! I was so excited that I ran the last 2.2 miles at a pace almost as fast as my one-mile time trials. Motivation success! I finished the race in 1:56:01, destroying my target of two hours and even beating that four-hour marathon equivalent time by seven seconds.

I found Chloe and Janet, sat down and snarfed some post-race snacks, and then got up to walk to a dim sum place half a block away.

I got there an hour later, after Chloe carried me to the first aid tent where I got iced down and gelled up, and where I stupidly refused crutches. My tent-to-dim-sum segment was run at a blistering three-hour-mile pace, which is roughly in the 0th percentile for males aged 20-29. My knees were burnt enchiladas, my right foot was a smoldering chorizo mash, and my left foot was an adorable Angora rabbit with all its bones replaced by thorns. I had barely felt any of this during the race, where I had apparently been landing too hard on my unprepared feet despite my trained toe-striking style[146].

I could hardly walk for four days, and it was another week before I could make the half mile to the grocery store to buy food, so I was living on meat sticks, dark chocolate, and tinned oysters for six days. It was twelve days before my left foot stopped hurting when standing. I continued to do non-weight-bearing exercises in the hopes that I would recover and be able to run the marathon, and I took the electric longboard down to see an active-release therapist who tortured my left calf and told me that I could try run-walking

---

145. "Those weren't Clif bars—they were special brownies! Welcome to The Haight!"
146. There must have been something wrong with my form, but it wasn't obvious what caused the damage.

the marathon if I loved death. With a week to go, I tried a slow, one-hour run and had to stop after fifty minutes from the pain.

Janet had been right: three months was too short. I decided that running the marathon was too hazardous, that I'd get stress fractures in my wimpy feet, and that run-walking a slow marathon would be anticlimactic. I didn't do the marathon, failing my goal. This was a big disappointment. I had been so psyched to see that my half marathon time indicated that my endurance was almost there after two months. I had done every exercise and stretched every stretch, but it wasn't enough.

My marathon goal ended in failure, but I realized that I'd fulfilled one of my reasons for training: to be able to run fast for a long time without tiring. I can't say that I've run a four-hour marathon, but I can go running whenever I want and enjoy it, which is something I've always wanted to be able to do and for which I have never been fit enough until now.

This marathon experience highlights for me the key question of when it's okay to give up on a goal and not do something that I said I would do. This should almost never happen, because every time it does, it weakens my Expectancy in myself to be able to do hard things in the future. If I can't trust myself not to make excuses for why it's okay to give up, then my motivation is going to take a big hit.

In this case, I knew in advance that I would have to skip the marathon if I got injured during training, but this injury seemed borderline. Was it medically necessary to quit, or was it overblown fear telling me not do it? I couldn't tell. I debated for days, made a cost/benefit analysis with all sorts of values for how likely I was to get how injured for how long versus how likely I would be to finish and how much that would be worth to me. I consulted friends and experts. Everything seemed to be a toss-up between run-walking it and not doing it at all, with a rough expected value of -$1400[147] for trying to run it quickly as I had wanted.

---

147. I converted possible results, like getting a stress fracture, to monetary values like -$2500, and multiplied them by probabilities, like 0.4, and added them all together to get a net expected value.

In the end, I think I made the right call. If you find yourself where I was, wondering whether it's okay to abandon a goal, then think thoroughly. The pain of having to finish a bad goal is often a fair price for the lesson on picking your goals. It's better to strengthen the habit of finishing goals, good and bad, than to cultivate the habit of quitting when it gets hard.

But don't break yourself.

5K

Run an official 5K in 23:15 from a pre-test of 28:15.

If I couldn't attempt the marathon, then I would crush the 5K[148]. I knew I was faster from the training, but how much? The last 5K trial had been at 25:52 ten weeks before. Had I improved another 2:37 since then? Could I maintain the 7:29 pace?

With Chloe, Janet, three other friends, and thousands of runners in white shirts, I lined up for the Color Me Rad 5K. This race had a twist: while you ran, they threw colored powder at you like in a Holi celebration, so that by the end you looked like a mutant rainbow puked on you.[149]

I ran as hard as I could, trying to break 23:15. When I finished, my phone told me 22:05. What?! There's no way I could have been *that* fast. From what the GPS told me, I suspect the course was only 4.62K. My best estimate of my extrapolated time is 23:32, which is 17 seconds short of my goal. 94% of the way. Worthwhile, but disappointing.

I would have felt a bit better about the time if I hadn't talked to my brother about it. He said that the last time he ran a 5K, just for kicks (he hadn't been training), that he ran it in just over 18 minutes by following this ex-military guy in front of him. He then lay gasping death on a picnic table for twenty minutes while the guy laughed and ran the 5K again to show off. It's a good thing I didn't

---

148. I registered for the 5K that was closest to the end of my project, which was a week later.

149. http://www.nickwinter.net/the-motivation-hacker/missions#5k

hear that story before all the training, or I wouldn't have placed as much Value in my goal of 23:15.

Now I have another goal. If I can drop my 5K time by another five minutes, I can compete with the past glory of my twin. It will take more than three months, but I will keep running.

Happiness

Hit average experiential happiness of 7.3 over the three months.
Here is my happiness tracking scale:

1: Suicidally depressed.

2: Majorly depressed or in tons of pain.

3: Frustrated or annoyed or sad or hurting or generally unhappy.

4: A little down.

5: Okay, I guess.

6: Happy.

7: Happy to the point of smiling or rocking out.

8: Excitedly happy; awesome.

9: Everything is just perfect.

10: Contender for best moment of my life.

I like to think of it as a logarithmic scale, or rather two logarithmic scales, where each point above five doubles my happiness and each point below five doubles my unhappiness. I have recorded my experiential happiness using this scale for the past two years, randomly each day an average of three times. This has taught me much about what makes me happy and unhappy.

But apart from filtering my music collection, I had never tried to optimize my happiness. I had never structured my day to have more happiness and less unhappiness; I had always just worked. Even when I did things like adventuring in Costa Rica, I still maintained my typical mean happiness of 6.00[150]. The highest average happiness was the previous 6.41 summer in Silicon Valley, where for the first time I found many people who were my people. Then I came back to Pittsburgh and worked harder than ever, averaging 6.26.

---

150. Standard deviation 1.0.

With this book, I aimed to crush that. I would leave no room in any days for not pursuing Value in all of the exciting, meaningful, and enjoyable missions I had lined up. I would have variety and vigor and would fear no negativity. I optimistically aimed to double my happiness, adding a whole point, to 7.3.

It did not work.

The first two months were good: 6.39 and 6.41. Not double-happiness great, but good: as happy as I had ever been. But then I finished my book draft early and had no glorious writing left to do, and worse, I was underchallenged with all that extra time in the day. I averaged only 5.90 for the last month. My overall average was 6.26: the same as when I did nothing but work on the Skritter iPhone app.

Through this project, I became better. I accomplished things which fueled my confidence, I learned skills I'll use the rest of my life, I got in shape, and I improved my relationships. All of my motivation hacking was successful, even if four of the uncontrollable results weren't quite what I wanted. But this fifth failure—the failure to be happier despite great effort to do so—this mark is black.

The psychological literature on well-being indicates that it's very hard to change one's happiness (apart from fixing problems like illness and poverty). Most attempts fail in acclimation and returns to baseline—you quickly get used to new states, and they stop making you happier. I thought that *I* could do it using my experiential sampling method and clever analysis to determine what could make me happiest. I had the freedom and motivation to structure my day however I liked. Why didn't it work?

I'm not sure. I am sorry. I wish I had, in this book, an answer for the question of how to live. It turns out I only have half an answer: how to do anything you want. The other half, figuring out what to want—that I don't know[151]. I'm young and naive, so I'll keep trying. If you have ideas for ways of living that can improve experiential happiness, let me know—I'll test them out.

---

151. Well, I do know that health is huge. Become healthy, feel better always. After health, though?

I opened this book with a quote from Walter Pater's *The Renaissance*[152]: "To burn always with this hard, gem-like flame, to maintain this ecstasy, is success in life." He is speaking of chasing passions and being present in every moment.[153] One cannot design a perfect life and then stop, for to treat any two moments alike is to live less.

I don't know what to do, but I aim to do as much of it as possible—and much is possible. I'll keep hacking motivation, and I'll keep burning, and I'll live a giant's life[154].

---

152. http://www.subir.com/pater/renaissance/conclusion.html
153. He then follows: "In a sense it might even be said that *our failure is to form habits*: for, after all, habit is relative to a stereotyped world, and meantime it is only the roughness of the eye that makes two persons, things, situations, seem alike. While all melts under our feet, we may well grasp at any exquisite passion, or any contribution to knowledge that seems by a lifted horizon to set the spirit free for a moment, or any stirring of the sense, strange dyes, strange colours, and curious odours, or work of the artist's hands, or the face of one's friend. Not to discriminate every moment some passionate attitude in those about us, and in the very brilliancy of their gifts some tragic dividing on their ways, is, on this short day of frost and sun, to sleep before evening."
154. One last motivation hack: a precommitment. If you know me and you see me living complacently, shame me. Remind me that I am to live a giant's life.

About the Author

Nick Winter was born, did nothing for eighteen years, and then had much catching up to do. After college, he said to his friends George and Scott, "Dudes, let's not get jobs and instead just start our own business." They pulled it off, and afterward Nick had to learn how to have a life. *The Motivation Hacker* is part of his answer.

Visit his website at http://www.nickwinter.net

Made in the USA
San Bernardino, CA
15 August 2017